SOLUTIONS MANUAL

OPTIONS, FUTURES, & OTHER DERIVATIVES

FOURTH EDITION

JOHN C. HULL

University of Toronto

PRENTICE HALL
Upper Saddle River, NJ 07458

Acquisitions editor: Paul Donnelly
Associate editor: Gladys Soto
Project editor: Richard Bretan
Manufacturer: Custom Printing Company

Printed in the United States of America

10   9   8   7   6   5

ISBN 0-13-014819-9

Prentice-Hall International (UK) Limited, London
Prentice-Hall of Australia Pty. Limited, Sydney
Prentice-Hall Canada Inc., Toronto
Prentice-Hall Hispanoamericana, S.A., Mexico
Prentice-Hall of India Private Limited, New Delhi
Prentice-Hall of Japan, Inc., Tokyo
Prentice-Hall (Singapore) Pte Ltd
Editora Prentice-Hall do Brasil, Ltda., Rio de Janeiro

Contents

Preface

This book contains solutions to the questions and problems that appear at the ends of chapters in my book *Options, Futures, and Other Derivatives*, 4th edition. The questions and problems (about 460 in total) have been designed to help readers study on their own and test their understanding of the material. They range from quick checks on whether a key point is understood to much more challenging applications of analytical techniques. To maximize the benefits from this book readers are urged to sketch out their own solutions to the problems before consulting mine.

I welcome comments on either *Options, Futures, and Other Derivatives*, 4th edition or this book. My e-mail address is

hull@mgmt.utoronto.ca

John C. Hull

CHAPTER 1
Introduction

1.1. When a trader enters into a long forward contract, she is agreeing to *buy* the underlying asset for a certain price at a certain time in the future. When a trader enters into a short forward contract, she is agreeing to *sell* the underlying asset for a certain price at a certain time in the future.

1.2. A trader is *hedging* when she has an exposure to the price of an asset and takes a position in a derivative to offset the exposure. In a *speculation* the trader has no exposure to offset. She is betting on the future movements in the price of the asset. *Arbitrage* involves taking a position in two or more different markets to lock in a profit.

1.3. In the first case the trader is obligated to buy the asset for \$50. (The trader does not have a choice.) In the second case the trader has an option to buy the asset for \$50. (The trader does not have to exercise the option.)

1.4. Writing a call option involves selling an option to someone else. It gives a payoff of

$$\min(X - S_T, 0)$$

Buying a put option involves buying an option from someone else. It gives a payoff of

$$\max(X - S_T, 0)$$

In both cases the potential payoff is $X - S_T$. When you write a call option, the payoff is negative or zero. (This is because the counterparty chooses whether to exercise.) When you buy a put option, the payoff is zero or positive. (This is because you choose whether to exercise.)

1.5. (a) The trader sells 100 million yen for \$0.0080 per yen when the exchange rate is \$0.0074 per yen. The gain is 100×0.0006 millions of dollars or \$60,000.
(b) The trader sells 100 million yen for \$0.0080 per yen when the exchange rate is \$0.0091 per yen. The loss is 100×0.0011 millions of dollars or \$110,000.

1.6. (a) The trader sells for 50 cents per pound something that is worth 48.20 cents per pound. Gain = $(\$0.5000 - \$0.4820) \times 50,000 = \$900$.
(b) The trader sells for 50 cents per pound something that is worth 51.30 cents per pound. Loss = $(\$0.5130 - \$0.5000) \times 50,000 = \$650$.

1.7. You have sold a put option. You have agreed to buy 100 IBM shares for \$120 per share if the party on the other side of the contract chooses to exercise his or her right to sell

1

for this price. The option will be exercised only when the price of IBM is below $120. If the counterparty exercises when the price is $110, you have to buy at $120 shares that are worth $110. You lose $10 per share or $1,000 in total. If the counterparty exercises when the price is $100, you lose $20 per share or $2,000 in total. The worst that can happen is that the price of IBM declines to zero during the 3-month period. This highly unlikely event would cost you $12,000. In return for the possible future losses you receive the price of the option from the purchaser.

1.8. One strategy would be to buy 200 shares. Another would be to buy 2,000 options. If the share price does well the second strategy will give rise to greater gains. For example, if the share price goes up to $40 you gain $[2,000 \times (\$40 - \$30)] - \$5,800 = \$14,200$ from the second strategy and only $200 \times (\$40 - \$29) = \$2,200$ from the first strategy. However, if the share price does badly, the second strategy gives greater losses. For example, if the share price goes down to $25, the first strategy leads to a loss of $200 \times (\$29 - \$25) = \$800$, whereas the second strategy leads to a loss of the whole $5,800 investment. This example shows that options contain built in leverage.

1.9. You could buy 5,000 put options (or 50 contracts) with a strike price of $25 and an expiration date in 4 months. This provides a type of insurance. If at the end of 4 months the stock price proves to be less than $25 you can exercise the options and sell the shares for $25 each. The cost of this strategy is the price you pay for the put options.

1.10. The trader makes a profit if the stock price is below $37 at the maturity of the option. The option will be exercised if the stock price is below $40. See Figure 1.1 for the variation of the profit with the stock price.

1.11 The trader makes a profit if the stock price is below $54 at the maturity of the option. The option will be exercised by the counterparty if the stock price is above $50. See Figure 1.2 for the variation of the profit with the stock price.

1.12. See Figure 1.3 for the variation of the trader's position with the asset price. We can divide the alternative asset prices into three ranges:
(a) When the asset price less than $40, the put option provides a payoff of $40 - S_T$ and the call option provides no payoff. The options cost $7 and so the total profit is $33 - S_T$.
(b) When the asset price is between $40 and $45, neither option provides a payoff. There is a net loss of $7.
(c) When the asset price greater than $45, the call option provides a payoff of $S_T - 45$ and the put option provides no payoff. Taking into account the $7 cost of the options, the total profit is $S_T - 52$.
The trader makes a profit (ignoring the time value of money) if the stock price is less than $33 or greater than $52. This type of trading strategy is known as a strangle and is discussed in Chapter 8.

2

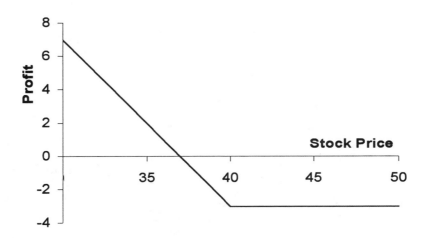

Figure 1.1   Profit from long put position in Problem 1.10

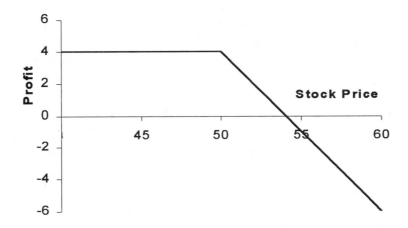

Figure 1.2   Profit from long put position in Problem 1.11

1.13. A stock option provides no funds for the company. It is a security sold by one trader to another. The company is not involved. By contrast, a stock when it is first issued is a claim sold by the company to investors and does provide funds for the company.

1.14. If a trader has an exposure to the price of an asset, she can hedge with a forward

3

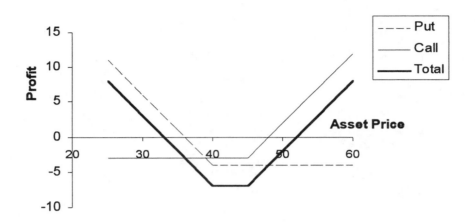

Figure 1.3 Profit from trading strategy in Problem 1.12

contract. If the exposure is such that the trader will gain when the price decreases and lose when the price increases, a long forward position will hedge the risk. If the exposure is such that the trader will lose when the price decreases and gain when the price increases, a short forward position will hedge the risk. Thus either a long or a short forward position can be entered into for hedging purposes. If the trader has no other exposure to the price of the underlying asset, entering into a forward contract is speculation.

1.15. Ignoring the time value of money, the holder of the option will make a profit if the stock price at maturity of the option is greater than $52.50. This is because the payoff to the holder of the option is, in these circumstances, greater than the $2.50 paid for the option. The option will be exercised if the stock price at maturity is greater than $50.00. Note that if the stock price is between $50.00 and $52.50 the option is exercised, but the holder of the option takes a loss overall. The profit from a long position is as shown in Figure 1.4.

1.16. Ignoring the time value of money, the seller of the option will make a profit if the stock price at maturity is greater than $56.00. This is because the cost to the seller of the option is in these circumstances less than the price received for the option. The option will be exercised if the stock price at maturity is less than $60.00. Note that if the stock price is between $56.00 and $60.00 the seller of the option makes a profit even though the option is exercised. The profit from the short position is as shown in Figure 1.5.

1.17. The trader receives an inflow of $2 in May. Since the option is exercised, the trader

4

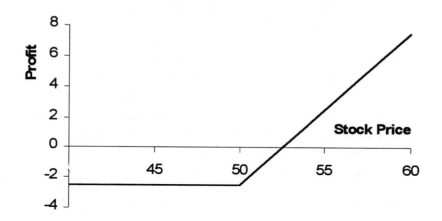

Figure 1.4 Profit from long position in Problem 1.15

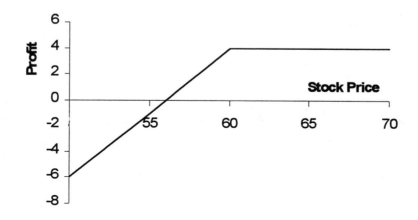

Figure 1.5 Profit from short position In Problem 1.16

also has an outflow of $5 in September. The $2 is the cash received from the sale of the option. The $5 is the result of buying the stock for $25 in September and selling it to the purchaser of the option for $20.

1.18. The trader makes a gain if the price of the stock is above $26 in December. (This

5

ignores the time value of money.)

1.19. A long position in a four-month put option can provide insurance against the exchange rate falling below the strike price. It ensures that the foreign currency can be sold for at least the strike price.

1.20. The company could enter into a long forward contract to buy 1 million Canadian dollars in six months. This would have the effect of locking in an exchange rate equal to the current forward exchange rate. Alternatively the company could buy a call option giving it the right (but not the obligation) to purchase 1 million Canadian dollar at a certain exchange rate in four months. This would provide insurance against a strong Canadian dollar in four months while still allowing the company to benefit from a weak Canadian dollar at that time.

1.21. The arbitrageur could borrow money to buy 100 ounces of gold today and short futures contracts on 100 ounces ounces of gold for delivery in one year. This means that gold is purchased for $500 per ounce and sold for $700 per ounce. The return (40% per annum) is far greater than the 10% cost of the borrowed funds. This is such a profitable opportunity that the arbitrageur should buy as many ounces of gold as possible and short futures contracts on the same number of ounces. Unfortunately arbitrage opportunities as profitable as this rarely arise in practice.

1.22. Most traders who use the contract will wish to do one of the following:
(a) Hedge their exposure to long-term interest rates,
(b) Speculate on the future direction of long-term interest rates, and
(c) Arbitrage between cash and futures markets.
This contract is discussed in Chapter 4.

1.23. The statement means that the gain (loss) to the party with a short position in an option is always equal to the loss (gain) to the party with the long position. The sum of the gains is zero.

1.24. The terminal value of the long forward contract is:

$$S_T - F_0$$

where S_T is the price of the asset at maturity and F_0 is the forward price of the asset at the time the portfolio is set up. (The delivery price in the forward contract is F_0.) The terminal value of the put option is:

$$\max\left(F_0 - S_T, 0\right)$$

The terminal value of the portfolio is therefore

$$S_T - F_0 + \max\left(F_0 - S_T, 0\right)$$

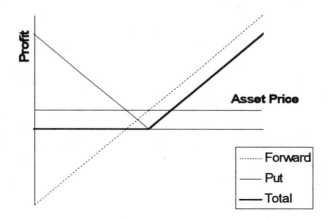

Figure 1.6 Payoff from portfolio in Problem 1.24

$$= \max (0, S_T - F_0]$$

This is the same as the terminal value of a European call option with the same maturity as the forward contract and an exercise price equal to F_0. This result is illustrated in the Figure 1.6.

1.25. Suppose that the value of the foreign currency (measured in \$U.S.) at maturity of the ICON is S_T and the payoff from the ICON is structured so that it is

$$1000 \quad \text{if} \quad S_T < X$$

$$1000 - \alpha(S_T - X) \quad \text{if} \quad X + \frac{1000}{\alpha} > S_T > X$$

$$0 \quad \text{if} \quad X + \frac{1000}{\alpha} < S_T$$

where α is a constant. In the example given in the text

$$\alpha = 169,000 \quad \text{and} \quad X = \frac{1}{169}$$

The payoff from an ICON is the payoff from:
(a) A regular bond
(b) A short position in α call options on the currency with exercise price X
(c) A long position in α call options on the currency with exercise price $X + \frac{1000}{\alpha}$
This is demonstrated by the following table

7

	Terminal Value of Regular Bond	Terminal Value of Short Calls	Terminal Value of Long Calls	Terminal Value of Whole Position
$S_T < X$	1000	0	0	1000
$X + \frac{1000}{\alpha} > S_T > X$	1000	$-\alpha(S_T - X)$	0	$1000 - \alpha(S_T - X)$
$S_T > X + \frac{1000}{\alpha}$	1000	$-\alpha(S_T - X)$	$\alpha(S_T - X - \frac{1000}{\alpha})$	0

1.26. Consider a range forward contract to buy one unit of a foreign currency. Suppose that S_T is the final exchange rate (value of one unit of the foreign currency) and the contract is structured so that
(a) If $S_T < X_1$, a price of X_1 is paid
(b) If $S_T > X_2$, a price of X_2 is paid
(c) If $X_1 \leq S_T \leq X_2$ the spot price is paid.
The range forward contract can be regarded as a short position in a put option with exercise price X_1 combined with a long position in a call option with exercise price X_2. This is demonstrated by the following table:

	Cost of Currency	Terminal Value of Put Position	Terminal Value of Call Position	Net Cost
$S_T < X_1$	$-S_T$	$-(X_1 - S_T)$	0	$-X_1$
$X_1 < S_T < X_2$	$-S_T$	0	0	$-S_T$
$X_2 < S_T$	$-S_T$	0	$S_T - X_2$	$-X_2$

The range forward contract is normally set up so that the initial value of the call equals the initial value of the put, that is, so that it costs nothing to set up the range forward contract. Note that when $X_1 = X_2$ a regular forward contract is obtained.

1.27. Suppose that the forward price for the contract entered into on July 1, 1999 is F_1 and that the forward price for the contract entered into on September 1, 1999 is F_2. If the value of one Japanese yen (measured in U.S. dollars) is S_T on January 1, 2000, then the value of the first contract (per yen bought) at that time is

$$S_T - F_1$$

while the value of the second contract (per yen sold) at that time is:

$$F_2 - S_T$$

The total payoff from the two contracts is therefore

$$S_T - F_1 + F_2 - S_T = F_2 - F_1$$

8

Thus if the forward price for delivery on January 1, 2000 increases between July 1, 1999 and September 1, 1999 the company will make a profit.

1.28. (a) The trader buys a 180-day call option and takes a short position in a 180 day forward contract. If S_T is the terminal spot rate, the profit from the call option is

$$\max\left(S_T - 1.57, \, 0\right) - 0.02$$

The profit from the short forward contract is

$$1.6018 - S_T$$

The profit from the strategy is therefore

$$\max\left(S_T - 1.57, \, 0\right) - 0.02 + 1.6018 - S_T$$

or

$$\max\left(S_T - 1.57, \, 0\right) + 1.5818 - S_T$$

This is

$$1.5818 - S_T \quad \text{when} \quad S_T < 1.57$$
$$0.0118 \quad\quad \text{when} \quad S_T > 1.57$$

This shows that the profit is always positive. The time value of money has been ignored in these calculations. However, when it is taken into account the strategy is still likely to be profitable in all circumstances. (We would require an extremely high interest rate for $0.0118 interest to be required on an outlay of $0.02 over a 180-day period.)

(b) The trader buys 90-day put options and takes a long position in a 90 day forward contract. If S_T is the terminal spot rate, the profit from the put option is

$$\max\left(1.64 - S_T, \, 0\right) - 0.020$$

The profit from the long forward contract is

$$S_T - 1.6056$$

The profit from this strategy is therefore

$$\max\left(1.64 - S_T, \, 0\right) - 0.020 + S_T - 1.6056$$

or

$$\max\left(1.64 - S_T, \, 0\right) + S_T - 1.6256$$

This is

$$S_T - 1.6256 \quad \text{when} \quad S_T > 1.64$$
$$0.0144 \quad\quad \text{when} \quad S_T < 1.64$$

The profit is therefore always positive. Again, the time value of money has been ignored but is unlikely to affect the overall profitability of the strategy. (We would require interest rates to be extremely high for $0.0144 interest to be required on an outlay of $0.02 over a 90-day period.)

CHAPTER 2
Futures Markets and the Use of Futures for Hedging

2.1. The *open interest* of a futures contract at a particular time is the total number of long positions outstanding. (Equivalently, it is the total number of short positions outstanding.) The *trading volume* during a certain period of time is the number of contracts traded during this period.

2.2. A *commission broker* trades on behalf of a client and charges a commission. A *local* trades on his or her own behalf.

2.3. The margin account administered by the clearinghouse is marked to market daily and the clearinghouse member is required to bring the account back up to the prescribed level daily. The margin account administered by the broker is also marked to market daily. However, it does not have to be brought up to the initial margin level on a daily basis. It has to be brought up to the initial margin level when the balance in the account falls below the maintenance margin level. The maintenance margin is about 75% of the initial margin.

2.4. The most important aspects of the design of a new futures contract are the specification of the underlying asset, the size of the contract, the delivery arrangements, and the delivery months.

2.5. A *margin* is a sum of money deposited by an investor with his or her broker. It acts as a guarantee that the investor can cover any losses on the futures contract. The balance in the margin account is adjusted daily to reflect gains and losses on the futures contract. If losses are above a certain level, the investor is required to deposit a further margin. This system makes it unlikely that the investor will default. A similar system of margins makes it unlikely that the investor's broker will default on the contract it has with the clearinghouse member and unlikely that the clearinghouse member will default with the clearinghouse.

2.6. A *short hedge* is appropriate when a company owns an asset and expects to sell it in the future. A *long hedge* is appropriate when a company knows it will have to purchase an asset in the future. It can also be used to offset the risk from an existing short position.

2.7. *Basis risk* arises from the hedger's uncertainty as to the difference between the spot price and futures price at the expiration of the hedge.

2.8. A perfect hedge is one that completely eliminates the hedger's risk. A perfect hedge does not always lead to a better outcome than an imperfect hedge. It just leads to a more certain outcome. Consider the situation where a company hedges its exposure to the price of an asset. Suppose the asset's price movements prove to be favorable to the company. A perfect hedge totally neutralizes the company's gain from these favorable price movements. An imperfect hedge, which only partially neutralizes these gains, might well work out better.

2.9. A minimum variance hedge leads to no hedging at all when the coefficient of correlation between the futures price and the price of the asset being hedged is zero.

2.10. There will be a margin call when \$1,000 has been lost from the margin account. This will occur when the price of silver increases by $1000/5000 = \$0.20$. The price of silver must therefore rise to \$5.40 per ounce for there to be a margin call. If the margin call is not met, the position is closed out.

2.11. These options make the contract less attractive to the party with the long position and more attractive to the party with the short position. They therefore tend to reduce the futures price.

2.12. There is a margin call if \$1,500 is lost on one contract. This happens if the futures price of frozen orange juice falls by 10 cents to 150 cents per lb. \$2,000 can be withdrawn from the margin account if the value of one contract rises by \$1,000. This will happen if the futures price rises by 6.67 cents to 166.67 cents per lb.

2.13. The clearinghouse member is required to provide $20 \times \$2,000 = \$40,000$ as initial margin for the new contracts. There is a gain of $(50{,}200 - 50{,}000) \times 100 = \$20{,}000$ on the existing contracts. There is also a loss of $(51{,}000 - 50{,}200) \times 20 = \$16{,}000$ on the new contracts. The member must therefore add

$$40{,}000 - 20{,}000 + 16{,}000 = \$36{,}000$$

to the margin account.

2.14. The optimal hedge ratio is

$$0.8 \times \frac{0.65}{0.81} = 0.642$$

This means that the size of the futures position should be 64.2% of the size of the company's exposure in a 3-month hedge.

2.15. Speculators are important market participants because they add liquidity to the market. However, contracts must have some useful economic purpose. Regulators generally only approve contracts when they are likely to be of interest to hedgers as well as speculators.

2.16. The most actively traded contracts as measured by the estimated volume of trading are

Grains and Oilseeds:	Corn (CBT)
Livestock and Meat:	Cattle-live (CME)
Food and Fiber:	Sugar-world (CSCE)
Metals and Petroleum:	Crude Oil (NYM)

2.17. The contract would not be a success. Parties with short positions would hold their contracts until delivery period and then deliver the cheapest form of the asset. Once news of the quality problem becomes widely known no one would be prepared to buy the contract. This shows that futures contracts are feasible only when there are rigorous standards within an industry for defining the quality of the asset. Many futures contracts have in practice failed because of the problem of defining quality.

2.18. If both sides of the transaction are entering into a new contract, the open interest increases by one. If both sides of the transaction are closing out existing positions, the open interest decreases by one. If one party is entering into a new contract while the other party is closing out an existing position, the open interest stays the same.

2.19. A good rule of thumb is to choose a futures contract that has a delivery month as close as possible to, but later than, the the month containing the expiration of the hedge. The contracts that should be used are therefore
(a) July
(b) September
(c) March

2.20. No. A perfect hedge aims to lock in the futures price.

2.21. The basis is the amount by which the spot price exceeds the futures price. A short hedger is long the asset and short futures contracts. The value of his or her position therefore improves as the basis increases. Similarly it worsens as the basis decreases.

2.22. The simple answer to this question is that the treasurer should
(i) Estimate the company's future cash flows in Japanese yen and U.S. dollars
(ii) Enter into forward and futures contracts to lock in the exchange rate for the U.S. dollar cash flows.
But this may not be the whole story. The company should examine whether the magnitudes of the foreign cash flows depend on the exchange rate. For example, will the company be able to raise the price of its product in U.S. dollars if the yen appreciates? If the company can do so its foreign exchange exposure may be quite low. The key estimates required are those showing the overall effect on the company's profitability of changes in the exchange rate at various times in the future. Once these estimates have been produced the company can choose between using futures and options to hedge its risk. The results of the analysis should be presented carefully

to other executives. It should be explained that a hedge does not ensure that profits will be higher. It means that profit will be more certain. When futures/forwards are used both the downside and upside are eliminated. With options a premium is paid to eliminate only the downside.

2.23. The statement is not true. The minimum variance hedge ratio is

$$\rho \frac{\sigma_S}{\sigma_F}$$

It is 1.0 when $\rho = 0.5$ and $\sigma_S = 2\sigma_F$. Since $\rho < 1.0$ the hedge is clearly not perfect.

2.24. The statement is true. Using the notation in the text, if the hedge ratio is 1.0, the hedger locks in a price of $F_1 + b_2$. Since both F_1 and b_2 are known this has a variance of zero.

2.25. The minimum variance hedge ratio is

$$0.7 \times \frac{1.2}{1.4} = 0.6$$

The beef producer requires a long position in $200000 \times 0.6 = 120,000$ lbs of cattle. The beef producer should therefore take a long position in 3 contracts.

2.26. The farmer can short 3 contracts which have 3 months to maturity. If the price of hogs fall, the gain on the futures contract will offset the loss on the sale of the hogs. If the price of hogs rise, the gain on the sale of the hogs will be offset by the loss on the futures contract. Using futures contracts to hedge has the advantage that it can at no cost reduce risk to almost zero. Its disadvantage is that the farmer no longer gains from favorable movements in hog prices.

2.27. The mining company can estimate its production on a month-by-month basis. It can then short futures contracts to lock in the price received for the gold. For example, if 3000 ounces are expected to be produced in November 1999 and December 1999, the price received for this production can be hedged by shorting a total of 30 December 1999 contracts.

2.28. What the airline executive says may be true. However, it can be argued that an airline is not in the business of forecasting the price of oil or of exposing its shareholders to the risk associated with the future price of oil. It should hedge and focus on its area of expertise.

2.29. If the company uses a hedge ratio of 1.5 in the example it would at each stage short 150 contracts. The gain from the futures contracts would be

$$1.50 \times 1.70 = \$2.55 \text{ per barrel}$$

13

and the company would be $0.85 per barrel better off.

2.30. This assumes that shareholders have as much information about the risks faced by a company as the company's management. In most instances, this is not the case. It also ignores commissions and other transactions costs. These are less expensive per dollar of hedging for large transactions than for small transactions. Hedging is therefore likely to be less expensive when carried out by the company than by individual shareholders. Indeed, the size of many futures contracts makes hedging by individual shareholders impossible in many situations.

There is another argument that can be used. One thing that shareholders can do far more easily than a corporation is diversify their risk. A shareholder with a well-diversified portfolio may be immune to many of the risks faced by a corporation. For example, in addition to holding shares in a company that uses copper, a well-diversified shareholder may well also hold shares in a copper producer. If companies are acting in the best interests of well-diversified shareholders, it can be argued that hedging is unnecessary in many situations.

2.31. If input price changes are passed on to the customer hedging is unnecessary. Whether price changes can be passed on to the customer without losing market share depends on the industry.

2.32. A hedge using futures contracts can result in a decrease or an increase in a company's profits relative to the position it would be in with no hedging. If a hedge improves profits the treasurer can then congratulate himself or herself on having had the foresight to put the hedge in place. Clearly the company is better off than it would be with no hedging. Other executives in the organization, it is hoped, will appreciate the contribution made by the treasurer. If the hedge leads to a reduction in profits (because a loss is made on the hedging instrument and a gain is made on the item being hedged), the treasurer may in practice have a difficult time justifying his or her actions. The problem is that hedging reduces risks for the company but may increase risks for the treasurer if others in the company do not fully understand what is being done. This emphasizes the importance of hedging strategies being approved at a high level within an organization and communicated clearly to all employees.

CHAPTER 3
Forward and Futures Prices

3.1. (a) The rate with continuous compounding is

$$4\ln\left(1 + \frac{0.14}{4}\right) = 0.1376$$

or 13.76% per annum.

(b) The rate with annual compounding is

$$\left(1 + \frac{0.14}{4}\right)^4 - 1 = 0.1475$$

or 14.75% per annum.

3.2. The investor's broker borrows the shares from another client's account and sells them in the usual way. To close out the position the investor must purchase the shares. The broker then replaces them in the account of the client from whom they were borrowed. The party with the short position must remit to the broker dividends and other income paid on the shares. The broker transfers the funds to the account of the client from whom the shares were borrowed. Occasionally the broker runs out of places from which to borrow the shares. The investor is then short squeezed and has to close out the position immediately.

3.3. The forward price is
$$30e^{0.12\times0.5} = \$31.86$$

3.4. The futures price is
$$350e^{(0.08-0.04)\times0.3333} = \$354.7$$

3.5. Gold is held for investment by some investors. If the futures price is too high, investors will find it profitable to increase their holdings of gold and short futures contracts. If the futures price is too low, they will find it profitable to decrease their holding of gold and go long in the futures market. Copper is a consumption asset. If the futures price is too high, a "buy copper and short futures" contract works. However, since investors do not in general hold the asset, the "sell copper and buy futures strategy" is not widely used when the futures price is low. There is therefore an upper bound but no lower bound to the futures price.

15

3.6. Convenience yield measures the extent to which there are benefits obtained from own-ership of the physical asset that are not obtained by owners of long futures contracts. The cost of carry is the interest cost plus storage cost less the income earned. The futures price, F_0, and spot price, S_0, are related by

$$F_0 = S_0 e^{(c-y)T}$$

where c is the cost of carry, y is the convenience yield, and T is the time to maturity of the futures contract.

3.7. The futures price of a stock index is always less than the expected future value of the index. This follows from the arguments in Section 3.12 and the fact that the index has positive systematic risk. Let μ be the expected return required by investors on the index so that $E(S_T) = S e^{(\mu-q)T}$ where E denotes expected value. Since $\mu > r$ and $F_0 = S_0 e^{(r-q)T}$, it follows that $E(S_T) > F_0$.

3.8. (a) With annual compounding the return is

$$\frac{1100}{1000} - 1 = 0.1$$

or 10% per annum.

(b) With semi-annual compounding the return is R where

$$1000 \left(1 + \frac{R}{2}\right)^2 = 1100$$

i.e.,

$$1 + \frac{R}{2} = \sqrt{1.1} = 1.0488$$

so that $R = 0.0976$. The percentage return is therefore 9.76% per annum.

(c) With monthly compounding the return is R where

$$1000 \left(1 + \frac{R}{12}\right)^{12} = 1000$$

i.e.,

$$\left(1 + \frac{R}{12}\right) = \sqrt[12]{1.1} = 1.00797$$

so that $R = 0.0957$ The percentage return is therefore 9.57% per annum.

(d) With continuous compounding the return is R where:

$$1000 e^R = 1100$$

16

i.e.,

$$e^R = 1.1$$

so that $R = \ln 1.1 = 0.0953$. The percentage return is therefore 9.53% per annum.

3.9. The rate of interest is R where:

$$e^R = \left(1 + \frac{0.15}{12}\right)^{12}$$

i.e.,

$$R = 12 \ln\left(1 + \frac{0.15}{12}\right)$$

$$= 0.1491$$

The rate of interest is therefore 14.91% per annum.

3.10. The equivalent rate of interest with quarterly compounding is R where

$$e^{0.12} = \left(1 + \frac{R}{4}\right)^4$$

or

$$R = 4(e^{0.03} - 1) = 0.1218$$

The amount of interest paid each quarter is therefore:

$$10000 \times \frac{0.1218}{4} = 304.55$$

or $304.55.

3.11. (a) The forward price, F_0, is given by equation (3.5) as:

$$F_0 = 40e^{0.1} = 44.21$$

or $44.21. The initial value of the forward contract is zero.

(b) The delivery price K in the contract is $44.21. The value of the contract, f, after six months is given by equation (3.9) as:

$$f = 45 - 44.21e^{-0.1 \times 0.5}$$

$$= 2.95$$

i.e., it is $2.95. The forward price is given by:

$$45e^{0.1 \times 0.5} = 47.31$$

17

or $47.31.

3.12. Using equation (3.7) the six month futures price is

$$150e^{(0.07-0.032)\times 0.5} = 152.88$$

or $152.88.

3.13. The futures contract lasts for five months. The dividend yield is 2% for three of the months and 5% for two of the months. The average dividend yield is therefore

$$\frac{1}{5}(3 \times 2 + 2 \times 5) = 3.2\%$$

The futures price is therefore

$$300e^{(0.09-0.032)\times 0.4167} = 307.34$$

or $307.34.

3.14. The theoretical futures price is

$$400e^{(0.10-0.04)\times 0.3333} = 408.08$$

The actual futures price is only 405. This shows that the index futures price is too low relative to the index. The correct arbitrage strategy is
(a) Go long futures contracts
(b) Short the shares underlying the index.

3.15. The settlement prices for the futures contracts are
    Sept 98   1.6318
    Dec 98   1.6242
    Jun 99   1.6096
The December futures is about 0.47% less than the September futures. The June futures is about 0.90% less than the December futures. Sterling seems to be becoming weaker in the futures market at about 0.45% per quarter or 1.8% per year. This suggests that sterling interest rates are higher than U.S. interest rates by about 1.8% per annum.

3.16. The theoretical futures price is

$$0.65e^{0.1667\times(0.08-0.03)} = 0.6554$$

The actual futures price is too high. This suggests that an arbitrageur should borrow U.S. dollars, buy Swiss francs, and short Swiss franc futures.

18

3.17. The present value of the storage costs for nine months are

$$0.06 + 0.06e^{-0.25 \times 0.1} + 0.06e^{-0.5 \times 0.1} = 0.176$$

or \$0.176. The futures price is from equation (3.15) given by F_0 where

$$F_0 = (9.000 + 0.176)e^{0.1 \times 0.75} = 9.89$$

i.e., it is \$9.89 per ounce.

3.18. If

$$F_2 > (F_1 + U)e^{r(t_2 - t_1)}$$

an investor could make a riskless profit by
(a) taking a long position in a futures contract which matures at time t_1
(b) taking a short position in a futures contract which matures at time t_2
When the first futures contract matures, an amount $F_1 + U$ is borrowed at rate r for time $t_2 - t_1$. The funds are used to purchase the asset for F_1 and store it until time t_2. At time t_2 it is exchanged for F_2 under the second contract. An amount $(F_1 + U)e^{r(t_2 - t_1)}$ is required to repay the loan. A positive profit of

$$F_2 - (F_1 + U)e^{r(t_2 - t_1)}$$

is, therefore, realized at time t_2. This type of arbitrage opportunity cannot exist for long. Hence:

$$F_2 \leq (F_1 + U)e^{r(t_2 - t_1)}$$

3.19. In total the gain or loss under a futures contract is equal to the gain or loss under the corresponding forward contract. However the timing of the cash flows is different. When the time value of money is taken into account a futures contract may prove to be more valuable or less valuable than a forward contract. Of course the company does not know in advance which will work out better. The long forward contract provides a perfect hedge. The long futures contract provides a slightly imperfect hedge.

(a) In this case, the forward contract leads to a slightly better outcome. The company takes a loss on its hedge. If a forward contract is used, the whole of the loss is realized at the end. If a futures contract is used, the loss is realized day by day throughout the contract. On a present value basis the former is preferable.

(b) In this case the futures contract leads to a slightly better outcome. The company makes a gain on the hedge. If a forward contract is used, the gain is realized at the end. If a futures contract is used, the gain is realized day by day throughout the life of the contract. On a present value basis the latter is preferable.

(c) In this case the futures contract leads to a slightly better outcome. This is because it gives rise to positive cash flows early and negative cash flows later.

(d) In this case the forward contract leads to a slightly better outcome. This is because, when a futures contract is used, the early cash flows are negative and the later cash flows are positive.

3.20. From equation (3.25) the forward exchange rate is an unbiased predictor of the future exchange rate when $r = k$. This is the case when the ex hange rate has no systematic risk.

3.21. In the foreign exchange futures market, prices are always quoted as number of U.S. dollars per unit of the foreign currency. In the spot and forward markets, prices are usually quoted the other way around: as the number of units of the foreign currency per U.S. dollar. The British pound and one or two other currencies are exceptions in that prices in the spot and forward markets are quoted in the same way as in the futures market.

3.22. The forward quote means that 1.8204 Swiss francs equal one U.S. dollar in the forward market. The futures quote means that 0.5479 U.S. dollars equals one Swiss franc in the futures market. When expressed in the same way (USD per Swiss franc) the quotes are 0.5493 and 0.5479 respectively. The forward quote is more favorable for an investor wanting to sell Swiss francs because it gives more USDs per Swiss franc.

3.23. When the geometric average of the price relatives is used, the changes in the value of the index do not correspond to changes in the value of a portfolio that is traded. Equation (3.12) is therefore no longer correct. The changes in the value of the portfolio is monitored by an index calculated from the arithmetic average of the prices of the stocks in the portfolio. Since the geometric average of a set of numbers is always less than the arithmetic average, equation (3.12) overstates the futures price. It is rumored that at one time (prior to 1988), equation (3.12) did hold for the Value Line Index. A major Wall Street firm was the first to recognize that this represented a trading opportunity. It made a financial killing by buying the stocks underlying the index and shorting the futures.

3.24. One S&P contract is on 250 times the index. The formula for the number of contracts that should be shorted gives

$$1.2 \times \frac{10,000,000}{900 \times 250} = 44.4$$

Rounding to the nearest whole number, 44 contracts should be shorted. To reduce the beta to 0.3, $44.4 \times 0.7 = 31$ contracts should be shorted.

3.25 The number of December futures contracts that should be shorted is

$$1.25 \times \frac{50,000 \times 30}{750 \times 500} = 5$$

20

3.26. When the convenience yield is high the futures price is much less than the current spot price. This makes it appear attractive to lock in the current futures price for an anticipated purchase. The real issue, though, is whether the futures price is less than the expected future spot price. This will often be the case, but it may not always be so. The arguments in Section 3.12 suggest that the relationship between the futures price and the expected future spot price depends on the systematic risk of the commodity.

3.27. (a) The relationship between the futures price F_1 and the spot price S_1 at time t_1 is

$$F_1 = S_1 e^{(r-r_f)(T-t_1)}$$

Suppose that the hedge ratio is h. The price obtained with hedging is

$$h(F_0 - F_1) + S_1$$

where F_0 is the initial futures price. This is

$$hF_0 + S_1 - hS_1 e^{(r-r_f)(T-t_1)}$$

If $h = e^{(r_f-r)(T-t_1)}$, this reduces to hF_0 and a zero variance hedge is obtained.

(b) When we are hedging over a very short period of time such as one day t_1 is close to zero and $h = e^{(r_f-r)T} = S_0/F_0$. The appropriate hedge ratio is therefore S_0/F_0.

(c) When a futures contract is used for hedging, the price movements in each day should in theory be hedged separately. This is because the contract is, in effect, closed out and rewritten at the end of each day. From (b) the correct hedge ratio at any given time is, therefore, S/F where S is the spot price and F is the futures price. Suppose there is an exposure to N units of the foreign currency and M units of the foreign currency underlie one futures contract. With a hedge ratio of 1 we should trade N/M contracts. With a hedge ratio of S/F we should trade

$$\frac{SN}{FM}$$

contracts. In other words we should calculate the number of contracts that should be traded as the dollar value of our exposure divided by the dollar value of one futures contract (This is not the same as the dollar value of our exposure divided by the dollar value of the assets underlying one futures contract.) Since a futures contract is settled daily we should in theory rebalance our hedge daily so that the outstanding number of futures contracts is always $(SN)/(FM)$. (In practice this is rarely done.)

3.28. Suppose that F_0 is the futures price at time zero for a contract maturing at time T and F_1 is the futures price for the same contract at time t_1. It follows that

$$F_0 = S_0 e^{(r-q)T}$$

$$F_1 = S_1 e^{(r-q)(T-t_1)}$$

where S_0 and S_1 are the spot price at times zero and t_1, r is the risk-free rate, and q is the dividend yield. These equations imply that

$$\frac{F_1}{F_0} = \frac{S_1}{S_0} e^{-(r-q)t_1}$$

Define the excess return of the index over the risk-free rate as x. The total return is $r + x$ and the return realized in the form of capital gains is $r + x - q$. It follows that $S_1 = S_0 e^{(r+x-q)t_1}$ and the equation for F_1/F_0 reduces to

$$\frac{F_1}{F_0} = e^{xt_1}$$

which is the required result.

CHAPTER 4
Interest Rates and Duration

4.1. Forward rates (with continuous compounding) for years two, three, four, and five are 7.0%, 6.6%, 6.4%, and 6.5%, respectively.

4.2. When the term structure is upward sloping $c > a > b$. When it is downward sloping $b > a > c$.

4.3. Consider a bond with a face value of $100. Its price is obtained by discounting the cash flows at 10.4% per year or 5.2% per six months. The price is

$$\frac{4}{1.052} + \frac{4}{1.052^2} + \frac{104}{1.052^3} = 96.74$$

If the 18-month spot rate is R we must have

$$\frac{4}{1.05} + \frac{4}{1.05^2} + \frac{104}{(1 + R/2)^3} = 96.74$$

which gives $R = 10.42\%$.

4.4. There are 89 days between October 12 and January 9 and 182 days between October 12, 2001 and April 12, 2001. The cash price of the bond is obtained by adding the accrued interest to the quoted price. It is

$$102.21875 + \frac{89}{182} \times 6 = 105.15$$

4.5. Cash price of Treasury bill is

$$100 - \frac{1}{4} \times 10 = 97.5$$

Continuously compounded return on an actual/actual basis is

$$\frac{365}{90} \ln \frac{100}{97.5} = 10.27\%$$

4.6. A duration-based hedging scheme assumes that term structure movements are always parallel. In other words it assumes that interest rates of all maturities always change by the same amount in a given period of time.

4.7. Value of a contract is $108.46875 \times 1,000 = 108,468.75$. The number of contracts that should be shorted is

$$\frac{6,000,000}{108,468.75} \times \frac{8.2}{7.6} = 59.7$$

Rounding to the nearest whole number, 60 contracts should be shorted.

4.8. The forward rates are as follows:

Year 2:	14.0%
Year 3:	15.1%
Year 4:	15.7%
Year 5:	15.7%

4.9. The forward rates are as follows

Qtr 2:	8.4%
Qtr 3:	8.8%
Qtr 4:	8.8%
Qtr 5:	9.0%
Qtr 6:	9.2%

4.10. The 6-month rate (with continuous compounding) is $2\ln(1 + 6/94) = 12.38\%$. The 12-month rate is $\ln(1 + 11/89) = 11.65\%$.
For the 1.5-year bond we must have

$$4e^{-0.1238 \times 0.5} + 4e^{-0.1165 \times 1.0} + 104e^{-1.5R} = 94.84$$

where R is the 1.5-year spot rate. It follows that

$$3.76 + 3.56 + 104e^{-1.5R} = 94.84$$

$$e^{-1.5R} = 0.8415$$

$$R = 0.115$$

or 11.5%. For the 2-year bond we must have

$$5e^{-0.1238 \times 0.5} + 5e^{-0.1165 \times 1.0} + 5e^{-0.115 \times 1.5} + 105e^{-2R} = 97.12$$

where R is the 2-year spot rate. It follows that

$$e^{-2R} = 0.7977$$

$$R = 0.113$$

or 11.3%.

4.11. A long position in two of the 4% coupon bonds combined with a short position in one of the 8% coupon bonds leads to the following cash flows

$$\text{Year } 0 : 90 - 2 \times 80 = -70$$

$$\text{Year } 10 : 200 - 100 = 100$$

since the coupons cancel out. The 10-year spot rate is therefore

$$\frac{1}{10} \ln \frac{100}{70} = 0.0357$$

or 3.57% per annum.

4.12. If long-term rates were simply a reflection of expected future short-term rates, we would expect the term structure to be downward sloping as often as it is upward sloping. (This is based on the assumption that half of the time investors expect rates to increase and half of the time investors expect rates to decrease). Liquidity preference theory argues that long-term rates are high relative to expected future short-term rates. This means that the term structure should be upward sloping more often than it is downward sloping.

4.13. The number of days between January 27, 2001 and May 5, 2001 is 98. The number of days between January 27, 2001 and July 27, 2001 is 181. The accrued interest is therefore

$$6 \times \frac{98}{181} = 3.2486$$

The quoted price is 110.5312. The cash price is therefore

$$110.5312 + 3.2486 = 113.7798$$

or $113.78.

4.14. The cheapest-to-deliver bond is the one for which

$$\text{Quoted Price} - \text{Futures Price} \times \text{Conversion Factor}$$

is least. Calculating this factor for each of the 4 bonds we get

$$\text{Bond 1: } 125.15625 - 101.375 \times 1.2131 = 2.178$$
$$\text{Bond 2: } 142.46875 - 101.375 \times 1.3792 = 2.652$$
$$\text{Bond 3: } 115.96875 - 101.375 \times 1.1149 = 2.946$$
$$\text{Bond 4: } 144.06250 - 101.375 \times 1.4026 = 1.874$$

Bond 4 is therefore the cheapest to deliver.

4.15. There are 177 days between February 4 and July 30 and 182 days between February 4 and August 4. The cash price of the bond is, therefore:

$$110 + \frac{177}{182} \times 6.5 = 116.32$$

The rate of interest with continuous compounding is $2\ln 1.06 = 0.1165$ or 11.65% per annum. A coupon of 6.5 will be received in 5 days (= 0.01366 years) time. The present value of the coupon is

$$6.5e^{-0.01366 \times 0.1165} = 6.490$$

The futures contract lasts for 62 days (= 0.1694 years). The cash futures price if the contract were written on the 13% bond would be

$$(116.32 - 6.490)e^{0.1694 \times 0.1165} = 112.02$$

At delivery there are 57 days of accrued interest. The quoted futures price if the contract were written on the 12% bond would therefore be

$$112.02 - 6.5 \times \frac{57}{184} = 110.01$$

Taking the conversion factor into account the quoted futures price should be:

$$\frac{110.01}{1.5} = 73.34$$

4.16. If the bond to be delivered and the time of delivery were known, arbitrage would be straightforward. When the futures price is too high, the arbitrageur buys bonds and shorts an equivalent number of bond futures contracts. When the futures price is too low, the arbitrageur sells bonds and buys an equivalent number of bond futures contracts.

Uncertainty as to which bond will be delivered introduces complications. The bond which appears cheapest-to-delivery now may not in fact be cheapest-to-delivery at maturity. In the case where the futures price is too high, this is not a major problem since the party with the short position (i.e., the arbitrageur) determines which bond is to be delivered. In the case where the futures price is too low, the arbitrageur's position is far more difficult since he or she does not know which bond to buy; it is unlikely that a profit can be locked in for all possible outcomes.

4.17. The forward rate is 9.0% with continuous compounding or 9.102% with quarterly compounding. The value of the FRA is therefore

$$[1,000,000 \times 0.25 \times (0.095 - 0.09102)]e^{-0.086 \times 1.25} = 893.56$$

or $893.56.

4.18. The forward interest rate for the time period between months 6 and 9 is 9% per annum. This is because 9% per annum for three months when combined with $7\frac{1}{2}$% per annum for six months gives an average interest rate of 8% per annum for the nine-month period.

For there to be no arbitrage the Treasury bill futures contract should lock an interest rate of 9% per annum for the period between 6 months and 9 months. Its price should therefore be

$$1,000,000e^{-0.09\times0.25} = 977,751$$

or \$977,751.

This analysis assumes no difference between forward and futures prices.

4.19 (a) The bond's price is

$$8e^{-0.11} + 8e^{-0.11\times2} + 8e^{-0.11\times3} + 8e^{-0.11\times4} + 108e^{-0.11\times5} = 86.80$$

(b) The bond's duration is

$$\frac{1}{86.80}\left[8e^{-0.11} + 2\times8e^{-0.11\times2} + 3\times8e^{-0.11\times3} + 4\times8e^{-0.11\times4} + 5\times108e^{-0.11\times5}\right]$$

$$= 4.256 \text{ years}$$

(c) Since, with the notation in the chapter

$$\Delta B = -BD\Delta y$$

the effect on the bond's price of a 0.2% decrease in its yield is

$$86.80 \times 4.256 \times 0.002 = 0.74$$

The bond's price should increase from 86.80 to 87.54.

(d) With a 10.8% yield the bond's price is

$$8e^{-0.108} + 8e^{-0.108\times2} + 8e^{-0.108\times3} + 8e^{-0.108\times4} + 108e^{-0.108\times5} = 87.54$$

This is consistent with the answer in (c).

4.20. Duration-based hedging schemes assume parallel shifts in the yield curve. Since the 12-year rate moves by less than the 4-year rate, the portfolio manager is likely to be over-hedged.

4.21. The company treasurer can hedge the company's exposure by shorting Eurodollar futures contracts. The Eurodollar futures position leads to a profit if rates rise and a loss if they fall.

The duration of the commercial paper is twice that of the Eurodollar deposit underlying the Eurodollar futures contract. From equation (4.6) the contract price of a Eurodollar futures contract is 980,000. The number of contracts that should be shorted is, therefore,

$$\frac{4,820,000}{980,000} \times 2 = 9.84$$

Rounding to the nearest whole number 10 contracts should be shorted.

4.22. The treasurer should short Treasury bond futures contract. If bond prices go down, this futures position will provide offsetting gains. The number of contracts that should be shorted is

$$\frac{10,000,000 \times 7.1}{91,375 \times 8.8} = 88.30$$

Rounding to the nearest whole number 88 contracts should be shorted.

4.23. The answer in Problem 4.22 is designed to reduce the duration to zero. To reduce the duration from 7.1 to 3.0 instead of from 7.1 to 0, the treasurer should short

$$\frac{4.1}{7.1} \times 88.30 = 50.99$$

or 51 contracts.

4.24. You would prefer to own the corporate bond. Under the 30/360 daycount convention there are 3 days between February 28, 2001 and March 1, 2001. Under the actual/actual (in period) day count convention, there is only one day. Therefore you would earn approximately three times as much interest by holding the corporate bond!

4.25. When the yield, y is expressed with a compounding frequency of m times per year, equation (4.7) becomes

$$B = \sum_{i=1}^{n} \frac{c_i}{(1 + y/m)^{mt_i}}$$

so that

$$\frac{\partial B}{\partial y} = -\sum_{i=1}^{n} \frac{c_i t_i}{(1 + y/m)^{mt_i+1}}$$

The bond's duration is

$$D = \frac{1}{B} \sum_{i=1}^{n} \frac{t_i c_i}{(1 + y/m)^{mt_i}}$$

It follows that

$$\frac{\partial B}{\partial y} = -\frac{BD}{1 + y/m}$$

so that for small Δy

$$\Delta B = -\frac{BD\Delta y}{1 + y/m}$$

Note that as m tends to infinity, so that y is expressed with continuous compounding, this becomes the result in equation (4.11).

4.26. Section 3.6 shows that when the the underlying asset in a futures contract is positively correlated with interest rates we expect the futures price of the asset to be higher than the forward price. In this case the underlying variable is a three-month interest rate. It is highly positively correlated to other short-term interest rates. The arguments in section 3.6 therefore show that the futures interest rate is higher than the forward interest rate.

4.27. In this case $\sigma = 0.011$, $t_1 = 6$, and $t_2 = 6.25$. The convexity adjustment is

$$\frac{1}{2} \times 0.011^2 \times 6 \times 6.25 = 0.002269$$

or about 23 basis points. The futures rate is 4.8% with quarterly compounding or 4.77% with continuous compounding. The forward rate is therefore 4.54% with continuous compounding.

CHAPTER 5
Swaps

5.1. Company A has an apparent comparative advantage in fixed rate markets but wants to borrow floating. Company B has an apparent comparative advantage in floating rate markets but wants to borrow fixed. This provides the basis for the swap. There is a 1.4% per annum differential between the fixed rates offered to the two companies and a 0.5% per annum differential between the floating rates offered to the two companies. The total (apparent) gain to all parties from the swap is therefore $1.4\% - 0.5\% = 0.9\%$ per annum. Since the bank gets 0.1% per annum of this, the swap should make each of A and B 0.4% per annum better off. This means that it should lead to A borrowing at LIBOR -0.3% and to B borrowing at 13%. The appropriate arrangement is therefore as shown in Figure 5.1.

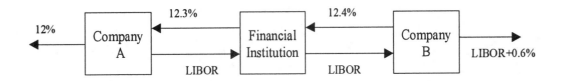

Figure 5.1   Swap for Problem 5.1

5.2. Company X has a comparative advantage in yen markets but wants to borrow dollars. Company Y has a comparative advantage in dollar markets but wants to borrow yen. This provides the basis for the swap. There is a 1.5% per annum differential between the yen rates and a 0.4% per annum differential between the dollar rates. The total gain to all parties from the swap is therefore $1.5\% - 0.4\% = 1.1\%$ per annum. Since the bank requires 0.5% per annum, this leaves 0.3% per annum for each of X and Y. The swap should lead to X borrowing dollars at $9.6 - 0.3 = 9.3\%$ per annum and to Y borrowing yen at $6.5\% - 0.3\% = 6.2\%$ per annum. The appropriate arrangement is therefore as shown in Figure 5.2. All foreign exchange risk is borne by the bank.

Figure 5.2   Swap for Problem 5.2

5.3. The swap rates imply that the LIBOR yield curve is flat at 10% with semiannual compounding. In 4 months $6 million will be received and $4.8 million will be paid.

In 10 months \$6 million will be received and the LIBOR rate prevailing in 4 months' time will be paid. The value of the fixed rate bond underlying swap is

$$6e^{-0.3333 \times 0.1} + 106e^{-0.8333 \times 0.1} = \$103.33 \text{ million}$$

The value of the floating rate bond underlying swap is

$$(100 + 4.8)e^{-0.3333 \times 0.1} = \$101.36 \text{ million}$$

The value of the swap to party paying floating is \$103.33 − \$101.36 = \$1.97 million. The value of the swap to party paying fixed is −\$1.97 million.

These results can also be derived by decomposing the swap into forward contracts. Consider the party paying floating. The first forward contract involves paying \$4.8 million and receiving \$6 million in 4 months. It has a value of $1.2e^{-0.3333 \times 0.1} = \$1.16$ million. To value the second forward contract we note that the forward interest rate is 10% per annum with continuous compounding or 10.254% per annum with semiannual compounding. The value of the forward contract is

$$100 \times (0.12 \times 0.5 - 0.10254 \times 0.5)e^{-0.0833 \times 0.1} = \$0.80 \text{ million}$$

The total value of the forward contract is therefore \$1.16 + \$0.80 = \$1.96 million.

5.4. The term "warehousing swaps" is used to refer to the situation where a financial institution does not enter into two offsetting swaps simultaneously. It makes a market in swaps and hedges the resultant risks.

5.5. The swap involves exchanging the sterling interest of $20 \times 0.14 = 2.8$ million for the dollar interest of $30 \times 0.1 = 3$ million. The principal amounts are also exchanged at the end of the life of the swap. The value of the sterling bond underlying the swap is:

$$\frac{2.8}{(1.11)^{1/4}} + \frac{22.8}{(1.11)^{5/4}} = 22.74 \text{ million}$$

The value of the dollar bond underlying the swap is

$$\frac{3}{(1.08)^{1/4}} + \frac{33}{(1.08)^{5/4}} = \$32.92 \text{ million}$$

Value of swap to party paying sterling is therefore

$$32.92 - 22.74 \times 1.65 = -\$4.60 \text{ million}$$

The value of the swap to the party paying dollars is +\$4.60 million.

The results can also be obtained by viewing the swap as a portfolio of forward contracts. The continuously compounded interest rates in sterling and dollars are 10.43% per annum and 7.70% per annum. The 3-month and 15-month forward exchange rates are $1.65e^{-0.25\times0.0273} = 1.6388$ and $1.65e^{-1.25\times0.0273} = 1.5946$. The value of the two forward contracts corresponding to the exchange of interest for the party paying sterling is therefore

$$(3 - 2.8 \times 1.6388)e^{-0.077\times0.25} = -\$1.56 \text{ million}$$

$$(3 - 2.8 \times 1.5946)e^{-0.077\times1.25} = -\$1.33 \text{ million}$$

The value of the forward contract corresponding to the exchange of principals is

$$(30 - 20 \times 1.5946)e^{-0.077\times1.25} = -\$1.72 \text{ million}$$

The total value of the swap is $-\$1.56 - \$1.33 - \$1.72 = -\$4.61$ million.

5.6. Credit risk arises from the possibility of a default by the counterparty. Market risk arises from movements in market variables such as interest rates and exchange rates.

5.7. At the start of the swap both contracts have a value of approximately zero. As time passes it is likely that this will change so that one swap has a positive value to the bank and the other has a negative value to the bank. If the counterparty on the other side of the positive-value swap defaults the bank still has to honor its contract with the other counterparty. It therefore loses an amount equal to the positive value of the swap.

5.8. The spread between the interest rates offered to X and Y is 0.8% per annum on fixed rate investments and 0.0% per annum on floating rate investments. This means that the total benefit to all parties from the swap is 0.8% per annum. Of this 0.2% per annum will go to the bank. This leaves 0.3% per annum for each of X and Y. In other words, company X should be able to get a fixed-rate return of 8.3% per annum while company Y should be able to get a floating-rate return LIBOR + 0.3% per annum. The required swap is shown in Figure 5.3. Company X has a net borrowing costs of LIBOR + 0.2% (or 0.3% per annum less than it would have if it went directly to floating rate markets).

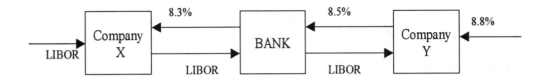

Figure 5.3   Swap for Problem 5.8

5.9. At the end of year 3 the financial institution was due to receive \$500,000 ($= 0.5 \times 10\%$ of \$10 million) and pay \$450,000 ($= 0.5 \times 9\%$ of \$10 million). The immediate loss is therefore \$50,000. We can assume that a swap where 6-month LIBOR is being exchanged for 8% per annum has zero NPV to the financial institution at the end of year 3. It follows that the default in effect costs the financial institution 2% per annum for the remaining life of the swap or 1% on each payment date. Hence the cost of default is:

year 3: $50,000
year $3\frac{1}{2}$: $100,000
year 4: $100,000
year $4\frac{1}{2}$: $100,000
year 5: $100,000

Discounting these cash flows to year 3 at 4% per six months we obtain the cost of the default as $413,000.

5.10. When rates are compounded annually the relationship between forward and spot rates is

$$F = S \left(\frac{1+r}{1+r_f} \right)^T$$

where F is the forward rate, S is the spot rate, r is the domestic risk-free rate, r_f is the foreign risk-free rate, and T is the time to maturity. Since $r = 0.08$ and $r_f = 0.03$, the spot and forward exchange rates at the end of year 6 are

spot: 0.8000
1 year forward: 0.8388
2 year forward: 0.8796
3 year forward: 0.9223
4 year forward: 0.9670

The effect of the default on the company's cash flows, measured in dollars, can be calculated as follows:

Year	Dollar Payment	Swiss Franc Payment	Forward Rate	Dollar Equivalent of Swiss Franc Payment	Cash Flow Lost
6	560,000	300,000	0.8000	240,000	(320,000)
7	560,000	300,000	0.8388	251,600	(308,400)
8	560,000	300,000	0.8796	263,900	(296,100)
9	560,000	300,000	0.9223	276,700	(283,300)
10	7,560,000	10,300,000	0.9670	9,960,100	2,400,100

Discounting the numbers in the final column to the end of year 6 at 8% per annum, the cost of the default is $679,800.

5.11. Company A has a comparative advantage in the Canadian dollar fixed-rate market. Company B has a comparative advantage in the U.S. dollar floating-rate market. However, company A wants to borrow in the U.S. dollar floating-rate market and company B wants to borrow in the Canadian dollar fixed-rate market. This gives rise to the swap opportunity.

The differential between the U.S. dollar floating rates is 0.5% per annum, and the differential between the Canadian dollar fixed rates is 1.5% per annum. The difference between the differentials is 1% per annum. The total potential gain to all parties from the swap is therefore 1% per annum, or 100 basis points. If the financial intermediary requires 50 basis points, each of A and B can be made 25 basis points better off. Thus a swap can be designed so that it provides A with U.S. dollars at LIBOR + 0.25% per annum, and B with Canadian dollars at 6.25% per annum. The swap is shown in Figure 5.4.

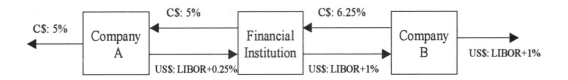

Figure 5.4   Swap for Problem 5.11

Principal payments flow in the opposite direction to the arrows at the start of the life of the swap and in the same direction as the arrows at the end of the life of the swap. The financial institution would be exposed to some foreign exchange risk which could be hedged using forward contracts.

5.12. The financial institution will have to buy 1.1% of the AUD principal in the forward market for each year of the life of the swap. Since AUD interest rates are higher than dollar interest rates, AUD is at a discount in forward markets. This means that the AUD purchased for year 2 is less expensive than that purchased for year 1; the AUD purchased for year 3 is less expensive than that purchased for year 2; and so on. This works in favor of the financial institution and improves its spread in future years.

5.13. A deferred swap can be regarded as a combination of two swaps which offset each other exactly for the first few years.
Consider for example a five-year swap to pay floating and receive fixed which will start in two years' time. This is a combination of
(a) A seven-year swap to pay floating and receive fixed
(b) A two-year swap to receive floating and pay fixed.
All other details of the swaps (e.g., the fixed rate of interest, frequency of payment, principal) are identical. Like other swaps, a deferred swap is usually constructed so that it has zero value initially. Note that this does not necessarily mean that each of the two swaps into which it can be decomposed has a zero value initially.

5.14. Consider a plain-vanilla interest rate swap involving two companies X and Y. We suppose that X is paying fixed and receiving floating while Y is paying floating and receiving fixed.

34

The quote suggests that company X will usually be less creditworthy than company Y. (Company X might be a BBB-rated company that has difficulty in accessing fixed-rate markets directly; company Y might be a AAA-rated company that has no difficulty accessing fixed or floating rate markets.) Presumably company X wants fixed-rate funds and company Y wants floating-rate funds.

The financial institution will realize a loss if company Y defaults when rates are high or if company X defaults when rates are low. These events are relatively unlikely since (a) Y is unlikely to default in any circumstances and (b) defaults are less likely to happen when rates are low. For the purposes of illustration, suppose that the probabilities of various events are as follows:

Default by Y:	0.001
Default by X:	0.010
Rates high when default occurs:	0.7
Rates low when default occurs:	0.3

The probability of a loss is

$$0.001 \times 0.7 + 0.010 \times 0.3 = 0.0037$$

If the roles of X and Y in the swap had been reversed the probability of a loss would be

$$0.001 \times 0.3 + 0.010 \times 0.7 = 0.0073$$

Assuming companies are more likely to default when interest rates are high, the above argument shows that the observation in quotes has the effect of decreasing the risk of a financial institution's swap portfolio. It is worth noting that the assumption that defaults are more likely when interest rates are high is open to question. The assumption is motivated by the thought that high interest rates often lead to financial difficulties for corporations. However, there is often a time lag between interest rates being high and the resultant default. When the default actually happens interest rates may be relatively low.

5.15. In an interest-rate swap a financial institution's exposure is the difference between a fixed-rate of interest and a floating-rate of interest. It has no exposure as far as the principal amount of the loan is concerned.

5.16. The bank is paying floating on the deposits and receiving fixed on the loans. It can offset its risk by entering into interest rate swaps (with other financial institutions or corporations) in which it contracts to pay fixed and receive floating.

5.17. The floating payments can be valued in currency A by (i) assuming that the forward rates are realized, and (ii) discounting the resulting cash flows at appropriate currency A discount rates. Suppose that the value is V_A. The fixed payments can be valued in currency B by discounting them at the appropriate currency B discount rates. Suppose that the value is V_B. If Q is the number of units of currency A per unit of currency B, the value of the swap in currency A is $V_A - QV_B$. Alternatively, it is $V_A/Q - V_B$ in currency B.

CHAPTER 6
Options Markets

6.1. When a trader buys an option, she must pay cash up front. There is no possibility of future liabilities and therefore no need for a margin account. When a trader sells an option, there are potential future liabilities. To protect against the risk of a default, margins are required.

6.2. On April 1, options trade with expiration months of April, May, August, and November. On May 30, options trade with expiration months of June, July, August and November. Longer maturity options are also sometimes traded.

6.3. The strike price is reduced to $20 and the option gives the holder the right to purchase 300 instead of 100 shares.

6.4. In the market maker/order book official system, an individual separate from the market maker keeps a record of limit orders and makes information on these orders available to traders. In the specialist system, a single individual acts as market maker and keeps a record of limit orders. Information on limit orders is not made available to other traders.

6.5. Writing a put gives a payoff of $\min(S_T - X, 0)$. Buying a call gives a payoff of $\max(S_T - X, 0)$. In both cases the potential payoff is $S_T - X$. The difference is that for a written put the counterparty chooses whether you get the payoff (and will allow you to get it only when it is negative). For a long put you decide whether you get the payoff and you choose to get it when it is positive.

6.6. Forward contracts lock in the exchange rate that will apply to a particular transaction in the future. Options provide insurance that the exchange rate will not be worse than some level. The advantage of a forward contract is that uncertainty is eliminated as far as possible. The disadvantage is that the outcome with hedging can be significantly worse than the outcome with no hedging. This disadvantage is not as marked with options. However, unlike forward contracts, options involve an up-front cost.

6.7. (a) The option contract becomes one to by $500 \times 1.1 = 550$ shares with an exercise price $40/1.1 = 36.36$.
(b) There is no effect. The terms of an options contract are not normally adjusted for cash dividends.
(c) The option contract becomes one to buy $500 \times 4 = 2,000$ shares with an exercise price of $40/4 = \$10$.

6.8. The exchange has certain rules governing when trading in a new option is initiated. These mean that the option is fairly close to being at-the-money when it is first traded. If all call options are in the money it is therefore likely that the stock price has risen since trading in the option began.

6.9. An unexpected cash dividend will reduce the stock price more than was expected. This will in turn reduce the value of a call option and increase the value of a put option.

6.10. (a) March, April, June and September
(b) July, August, September, December
(c) August, September, December, March
Longer dated options may also trade.

6.11. A "fair" price for the option can reasonably be assumed to be half way between the bid and the ask price. An investor typically buys at the ask and sells at the bid. Each time she does this there is a hidden cost equal to half the bid-ask spread.

6.12. The two calculations are necessary to determine the initial margin. The first gives are

$$500 \times (3.5 + 0.2 \times 57 - 3) = 5,950$$

The second gives
$$500 \times (3.5 + 0.1 \times 57) = 4,600$$

The initial margin is the greater of these, or \$5,950. Part of this can be provided by the initial amount of $500 \times 35 = \$1,750$ received for the options.

CHAPTER 7
Properties of Stock Option Prices

7.1. The investor's payoff is

$$\max(S_T - X,\, 0) + \min(S_T - X,\, 0) = S_T - X$$

The position is therefore equivalent to a long forward contract where the delivery price is X. When X equals the forward price the long forward contract is worth zero. It follows that the call and the put are equally valuable in this case.

7.2. The holder of an American option has all the rights that the holder of a similar European option and the right to exercise early. The American option must therefore be worth at least as much as the corresponding European option.

7.3. The holder of an American option has the option of exercising immediately and realizing the intrinsic value. It follows that the American option must be worth at least its intrinsic value.

7.4. The six factors affecting stock option prices are the stock price, strike price, risk-free interest rate, volatility, time to maturity, and dividends.

7.5. The lower bound is

$$28 - 25e^{-0.08 \times 0.3333} = \$3.66$$

7.6. The lower bound is

$$15e^{-0.06 \times 0.08333} - 12 = \$2.93$$

7.7. Delaying exercise delays the payment of the strike price. This means that the option holder is able to earn interest on the strike price for a longer period of time. Delaying exercise also provides insurance against the stock price falling below the strike price by the expiration date. Assume that the option holder has an amount of cash X and interest rates are zero. Exercising early means that the option holder's position will be worth S_T at expiration. Delaying exercise means that it will be worth $\max(X,\, S_T)$ at expiration.

7.8. An American put when held in conjunction with the underlying stock provides insurance. It guarantees that the stock can be sold for the strike price, X. If the put is exercised early, the insurance ceases. However, the option holder receives the strike price immediately. He or she is able to earn interest on X between the time of the early exercise and the expiration date.

7.9. When early exercise is not possible we can argue that two portfolios that are worth the same at time T must be worth the same at earlier times. When early exercise is possible, the argument falls down. Suppose that $P + S_0 > C + Xe^{-rT}$. This does not lead to an arbitrage opportunity. If we buy the call, short the put, and short the stock, we cannot be sure of the result since we cannot be sure when the put will be exercised.

7.10. The lower bound is

$$80 - 75e^{-0.1 \times 0.5} = \$8.66$$

7.11. The lower bound is

$$65e^{-0.1667 \times 0.05} - 58 = \$6.46$$

7.12. The present value of the strike price is $60e^{-0.3333 \times 0.12} = \$57.65$. The present value of the dividend is $0.80e^{-0.08333 \times 0.12} = 0.79$. Since

$$5 < 64 - 57.65 - 0.79$$

the condition in equation (7.5) is violated. An arbitrageur should buy the option and short the stock. Regardless of what happens a profit will materialize. If the stock price declines below \$60, the arbitrageur loses the \$5 spent on the option but gains at least $64 - 57.65 - 0.79 = \$5.56$ in present value terms from the short position. If the stock price is above \$60 at the expiration of the option, the arbitrageur gains in present value terms exactly $5.56 - 5.00 = \$0.56$.

7.13. In this case the present value of the strike price is $50e^{-0.08333 \times 0.06} = 49.75$ Since

$$2.5 < 49.75 - 47.00$$

the condition in equation (7.2) is violated. An arbitrageur can lock in a profit of at least \$0.25 by buying the put option and buying the stock.

7.14. The early exercise of an American put is attractive when the interest earned on the strike price is greater than the insurance element lost. When interest rates increase, the interest earned on the strike price increases making early exercise more attractive. When volatility decreases, the insurance element is less valuable. Again this makes early exercise more attractive.

7.15. Using the notation in the chapter, put-call parity gives [see equation (7.8)]

$$c + Xe^{-rT} + D = p + S_0$$

or

$$p = c + Xe^{-rT} + D - S_0$$

In this case

$$p = 2 + 30e^{-0.5 \times 0.1} + 0.5e^{-0.1667 \times 0.1} + 0.5e^{-0.4167 \times 0.1} - 29 = 2.51$$

In other words the put price is $2.51.

7.16. If the put price is $3.00, it is too high relative to the call price. An arbitrageur should buy the call, short the put and short the stock. Regardless of what happens this locks in a profit which has a present value of $3.00 - 2.51 = \$0.49$.

7.17. From equation (7.4)

$$S_0 - X < C - P < S_0 - Xe^{-rT}$$

In this case

$$31 - 30 < 4 - P < 31 - 30e^{-0.08 \times 0.25}$$

or

$$1.00 < 4.00 - P < 1.59$$

or

$$2.41 < P < 3.00$$

Upper and lower bounds for the price of an American put are therefore $2.41 and $3.00.

7.18. If the American put price is greater than $3.00 an arbitrageur can sell the American put, short the stock, and buy the American call. This realizes at least $3 + 31 - 4 = \$30$ which can be invested at the risk-free interest rate. At some stage during the 3-month period either the American put or the American call will be exercised. The arbitrageur then pays $30, receives the stock and closes out the short position for a profit.

7.19 As in the text we use c and p to denote the European call and put option price, and C and P to denote the American call and put option prices. Since $P > p$, it follows from put–call parity that

$$P > c + Xe^{-rT} - S_0$$

and since $c = C$,

$$P > C + Xe^{-rT} - S_0$$

or

$$C - P < S_0 - Xe^{-rT}$$

For a further relationship between C and P, consider
  Portfolio I: One European call option plus an amount of cash equal to X.
  Portfolio J: One American put option plus one share.
Both options have the same exercise price and expiration date. Assume that the cash in portfolio I is invested at the risk-free interest rate. If the put option is not exercised early portfolio J is worth

$$\max(S_T, X)$$

at time T. Portfolio I is worth

$$\max(S_T - X, 0) + Xe^{rT} = \max(S_T, X) - X + Xe^{rT}$$

at this time. Portfolio I is therefore worth more than portfolio J. Suppose next that the put option in portfolio J is exercised early, say, at time τ. This means that portfolio J is worth X at time τ. However, even if the call option were worthless, portfolio I would be worth $Xe^{r\tau}$ at time τ. It follows that portfolio I is worth more than portfolio J in all circumstances. Hence

$$c + X > P + S_0$$

Since $c = C$,

$$C + X > P + S_0$$

or

$$C - P > S_0 - X$$

Combining this with the other inequality derived above for $C - P$, we obtain

$$S_0 - X < C - P < S_0 - Xe^{-rT}$$

7.20. As in the text we use c and p to denote the European call and put option price, and C and P to denote the American call and put option prices. The present value of the dividends will be denoted by D. As shown in the answer to Problem 7.19, when there are no dividends

$$C - P < S_0 - Xe^{-rT}$$

Dividends reduce C and increase P. Hence this relationship must also be true when there are dividends.

For a further relationship between C and P, consider

Portfolio I: one European call option plus an amount of cash equal to $D + X$

Portfolio J: one American put option plus one share

Both options have the same exercise price and expiration date. Assume that the cash in portfolio I is invested at the risk-free interest rate. If the put option is not exercised early, portfolio J is worth

$$\max(S_T, X) + De^{rT}$$

at time T. Portfolio I is worth

$$\max(S_T, 0) + (D + X)e^{rT} = \max(S_T, X) + De^{rT} + X(e^{rT} - X)$$

at this time. Portfolio I is therefore worth more than portfolio J. Suppose next that the put option in portfolio J is exercised early, say, at time τ. This means that portfolio J is worth at most $X + De^{r\tau}$ at time τ. However, even if the call option were worthless, portfolio I would be worth $(D + X)e^{r\tau}$ at time τ. It follows that portfolio I is worth more than portfolio J in all circumstances. Hence

$$c + D + X > P + S_0$$

41

7.21. Executive stock options may be exercised early because the executive needs the cash or because she is uncertain about the company's future prospects. Regular call options can be sold in the market in either of these two situations, but executive stock options cannot be sold. In theory an executive can short the company's stock as an alternative to exercising. In practice this is not usually encouraged and may even be illegal.

CHAPTER 8
Trading Strategies Involving Options

8.1. A protective put consists of a long position in a put option combined with a long position in the underlying shares. It is equivalent to a long position in a call option plus a certain amount of cash. This follows from put-call parity:

$$p + S = c + Xe^{-rT} + D$$

8.2. A bear spread can be created using two call options with the same maturity and different strike prices. The investor shorts the call option with the lower strike price and buys the call option with the higher strike price. A bear spread can also be created using two put options with the same maturity and different strike prices. In this case the investor shorts the put option with the lower strike price and buys the put option with the higher strike price.

8.3. A butterfly spread involves a position in options with three different strike prices $(X_1, X_2,$ and $X_3)$. An investor should purchase a butterfly spread when it is considered that the price of the underlying stock is likely to stay close to the central strike price, X_2.

8.4. An investor can create a butterfly spread by buying call options with strike prices of \$15 and \$20, and selling two call options with strike prices of \$17$\frac{1}{2}$. The initial investment is $4 + \frac{1}{2} - 2 \times 2 = \$\frac{1}{2}$. The following table shows the variation of profit with the final stock price:

Stock Price S_T	Profit
$S_T < 15$	$-\frac{1}{2}$
$15 < S_T < 17\frac{1}{2}$	$S_T - 15\frac{1}{2}$
$17\frac{1}{2} < S_T < 20$	$19\frac{1}{2} - S_T$
$S_T > 20$	$-\frac{1}{2}$

8.5. A reverse calendar spread is created by buying a short-maturity option and selling a long-maturity option, both with the same strike price.

8.6. Both a straddle and a strangle are created by combining a call and a put. In a straddle they have the same strike price and expiration date. In a strangle they have different strike prices and the same expiration date.

8.7. A strangle is created by buying both options. The pattern of profits is as follows:

Stock Price S_T	Profit
$S_T < 45$	$40 - S_T$
$45 < S_T < 50$	-5
$S_T > 50$	$S_T - 55$

8.8. A bull spread using calls provides a profit pattern with the same general shape as a bull spread using puts (see Figures 8.2 and 8.3 in the text). Define p_1 and c_1 as the prices of put and call with strike price X_1 and p_2 and c_2 as the prices of a put and call with strike price X_2. From put-call parity

$$p_1 + S = c_1 + X_1 e^{-rT}$$

$$p_2 + S = c_2 + X_2 e^{-rT}$$

Hence:

$$p_1 - p_2 = c_1 - c_2 - (X_2 - X_1)e^{-rT}$$

This shows that the initial investment when the spread is created from puts is less than the initial investment when it is created from calls by an amount $(X_2 - X_1)e^{-rT}$. In fact as mentioned in the text the initial investment when the bull spread is created from puts is negative, while the initial investment when it is created from calls is positive.

The profit when calls are used to create the bull spread is higher than when puts are used by $(X_2 - X_1)(1 - e^{-rT})$. This reflects the fact that the call strategy involves an additional risk-free investment of $(X_2 - X_1)e^{-rT}$ over the put strategy. This earns interest of $(X_2 - X_1)(1 - e^{-rT})$.

8.9. An aggressive bull spread using call options is discussed in the text. Both of the options used have relatively high strike prices. Similarly, an aggressive bear spread can be created using put options. Both of the options should be out of the money (that is, they should have relatively low strike prices). The spread then costs very little to set up since both of the puts are worth close to zero. In most circumstances the spread will be worth zero. However, there is a small chance that the stock price will fall fast so that on expiration both options will be in the money. The spread is then worth the difference between the two strike prices $X_2 - X_1$.

8.10. A bull spread is created by buying the $30 put and selling the $35 put. This strategy gives rise to an initial cash inflow of $3. The outcome is as follows:

Stock Price	Payoff	Profit
$S_T \geq 35$	0	3
$30 \leq S_T < 35$	$S_T - 35$	$S_T - 32$
$S_T < 30$	-5	-2

A bear spread is created by selling the $30 put and buying the $35 put. This strategy costs $3 initially. The outcome is as follows:

Stock Price	Payoff	Profit
$S_T \geq 35$	0	-3
$30 \leq S_T < 35$	$35 - S_T$	$32 - S_T$
$S_T < 30$	5	2

8.11. Define c_1, c_2, and c_2 as the prices of calls with strike prices X_1, X_2 and X_3. Define p_1, p_2 and p_3 as the prices of puts with strike prices X_1, X_2 and X_3. With the usual notation

$$c_1 + X_1 e^{-rT} = p_1 + S$$

$$c_2 + X_2 e^{-rT} = p_2 + S$$

$$c_3 + X_3 e^{-rT} = p_3 + S$$

Hence

$$c_1 + c_3 - 2c_2 + (X_1 + X_3 - 2X_2)e^{-rT} = p_1 + p_3 - 2p_2$$

Since $X_2 - X_1 = X_3 - X_2$, it follows that $X_1 + X_3 - 2X_2 = 0$ and

$$c_1 + c_3 - 2c_2 = p_1 + p_3 - 2p_2$$

The cost of a butterfly spread created using European calls is therefore exactly the same as the cost of a butterfly spread created using European puts.

8.12. A straddle is created by buying both the call and the put. This strategy costs $10. The profit/loss is shown in the following table:

Stock Price	Payoff	Profit
$S_T > 60$	$S_T - 60$	$S_T - 70$
$S_T \leq 60$	$60 - S_T$	$50 - S_T$

This shows that the straddle will lead to a loss if the final stock price is between $50 and $70.

8.13. The bull spread is created by buying a put with strike price X_1 and selling a put with strike price X_2. The payoff is calculated as follows:

Stock Price Range	Payoff from Long Put Option	Payoff from Short Put Option	Total Payoff
$S_T \geq X_2$	0	0	0
$X_1 < S_T < X_2$	0	$S_T - X_2$	$-(X_2 - S_T)$
$S_T \leq X_1$	$X_1 - S_T$	$S_T - X_2$	$-(X_2 - X_1)$

8.14. Possible strategies are:

Strangle
Straddle
Strip
Strap
Reverse calendar spread
Reverse butterfly spread

The strategies all provide positive profits when there are large stock price moves. A strangle is less expensive than a straddle, but requires a bigger move in the stock price in order to provide a positive profit. Strips and straps are more expensive than straddles but provide bigger profits in certain circumstances. A strip will provide a bigger profit when there is a large downward stock price move. A strap will provide a bigger profit when there is a large upward stock price move. In the case of strangles, straddles, strips and straps, the profit increases as the size of the stock price movement increases. By contrast in a reverse calendar spread and a reverse butterfly spread there is a maximum potential profit regardless of the size of the stock price movement.

8.15. Suppose that the delivery price is K and the delivery date is T. The forward contract is created by buying a European call and selling a European put when both options have strike price K and exercise date T. It is easy to see that this portfolio provides a payoff of $S_T - K$ under all circumstances where S_T is the stock price at time T. Suppose that F is the forward price. If $K = F$, the forward contract that is created has zero value. This shows that the price of a call equals the price of a put when the strike price is K.

8.16. The bull spread involves buying a European call with strike price X_1 and selling a European call with strike price X_2. The bear spread involves buying a European put

46

with strike price X_2 and selling a European put with strike price X_1. The payoff from a box spread is shown in the following table:

Stock Price Range	Bull Call Spread	Bear Put Spread	Total
$S_T \geq X_2$	$X_2 - X_1$	0	$X_2 - X_1$
$X_1 < X_T < X_2$	$S_T - X_1$	$X_2 - S_T$	$X_2 - X_1$
$S_T \leq X_1$	0	$X_2 - X_1$	$X_2 - X_1$

It can be seen that under all circumstances the box spread pays off $X_2 - X_1$. If there are to be no arbitrage opportunities, the value of the box spread today must be the present value of $X_2 - X_1$.

8.17. The result is shown in Figure 8.1. The initial investment required is much higher but the profit pattern is very similar.

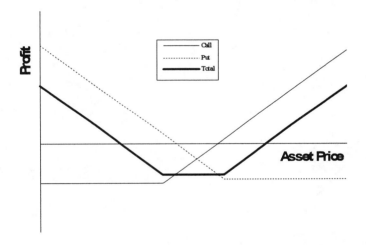

Figure 8.1   Profit Pattern in Problem 8.17

8.18. DerivaGem shows that the values of calls with strike prices of 0.60, 0.65, and 0.70 are 0.0618, 0.0352, and 0.0181. The values of puts with these three strike prices are 0.0176, 0.0386, and 0.0690. The cost of setting up the butterfly spread when calls are used is therefore

$$0.0618 + 0.0181 - 2 \times 0.0352 = 0.0095$$

47

The cost of setting up the butterfly spread when puts are used is

$$0.0176 + 0.0690 - 2 \times 0.0386 = 0.0094$$

Allowing for rounding errors these two are the same.

CHAPTER 9
Introduction To Binomial Trees

9.1. Consider a portfolio consisting of

-1 :   call option
$+\Delta$:   shares

If the stock price rises to \$42, this is worth $42\Delta - 3$. If the stock price falls to \$38, it is worth 38Δ. These are the same when

$$42\Delta - 3 = 38\Delta$$

or $\Delta = 0.75$. The value of the portfolio in one month is \$28.5 for both stock prices. Its value today must be the present value of 28.5 or $28.5e^{-0.08 \times 0.08333} = 28.31$. This means that

$$-f + 40\Delta = 28.31$$

where f is the call price. Since $\Delta = 0.75$, the call price is $40 \times 0.75 - 28.31$ or \$1.69. As an alternative approach, we can calculate the probability, p, of an up movement in a risk-neutral world. This must satisfy:

$$42p + 38(1-p) = 40e^{0.08 \times 0.08333}$$

so that

$$4p = 40e^{0.08 \times 0.08333} - 38$$

or $p = 0.5669$. The value of the option is then its expected payoff discounted at the risk-free rate or

$$(3 \times 0.5669 + 0 \times 0.4331)e^{-0.08 \times 0.08333} = 1.69$$

This agrees with the previous calculation.

9.2. In the no-arbitrage approach, we set up a riskless portfolio consisting of a position in the option and a position in the stock. By setting the return on the portfolio equal to the risk-free interest rate, we are able to value the option. When we use risk-neutral valuation, we first choose probabilities for the branches of the tree so that the expected return on the stock equals the risk-free interest rate. We then value the option by calculating its expected payoff and discounting this expected payoff at the risk-free interest rate.

9.3. The delta of a stock option measures the sensitivity of the option price to the price of the stock when small changes are considered. Specifically, it is the ratio of the change in the price of the stock option to the change in the price of the underlying stock.

9.4. Consider a portfolio consisting of

-1 :	put option
$+\Delta$:	shares

If the stock price rises to $55, this is worth 55Δ. If the stock price falls to $45, it is worth $45\Delta - 5$. These are the same when

$$45\Delta - 5 = 55\Delta$$

or $\Delta = -0.50$. The value of the portfolio in one month is -27.5 for both stock prices. Its value today must be the present value of -27.5 or $-27.5e^{-0.1 \times 0.5} = -26.16$. This means that

$$-pp + 50\Delta = -26.16$$

where pp is the put price. Since $\Delta = -0.50$, the put price is $1.16. As an alternative approach we can calculate the probability, p, of an up movement in a risk-neutral world. This must satisfy:

$$55p + 45(1 - p) = 50e^{0.1 \times 0.5}$$

so that

$$10p = 50e^{0.1 \times 0.5} - 45$$

or $p = 0.7564$. The value of the option is then its expected payoff discounted at the risk-free rate or

$$(0 \times 0.7564 + 5 \times 0.2436)e^{-0.1 \times 0.5} = 1.16$$

This agrees with the previous calculation.

9.5. In this case $u = 1.10$, $d = 0.90$, and $r = 0.08$ so that

$$p = \frac{e^{0.08 \times 0.5} - 0.90}{1.10 - 0.90} = 0.7041$$

The tree for stock price movements is shown in Figure 9.1. We can work back from the end of the tree to the beginning as indicated in the diagram to give the value of the option as $9.61. The option value can also be calculated directly from Equation (9.8):

$$e^{-2 \times 0.08 \times 0.5}(0.7041^2 \times 21 + 2 \times 0.7041 \times 0.2959 \times 0 + 0.2959^2 \times 0) = 9.61$$

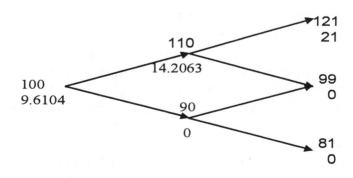

Figure 9.1 Tree for Problem 9.5

50

9.6. Figure 9.2 shows how we can value the put option using the same tree as in Figure 9.1. The value of the option is \$1.92. The option value can also be calculated directly from Equation (9.8):

$$e^{-2\times0.5\times0.08}[0.7041^2 \times 0 + 2 \times 0.7041 \times 0.2959 \times 1 + 0.2959^2 \times 19] = 1.92$$

The stock price plus the put price is $100 + 1.92 = 101.92$. The present value of the strike price plus the call price is $100e^{-0.08} + 9.61 = 101.92$. These are the same, verifying that put–call parity holds.

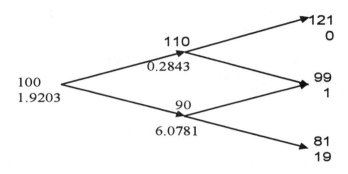

Figure 9.2   Tree for Problem 9.6

9.7. The riskless portfolio consists of a short position in the option and a long position in Δ shares. Since Δ changes during the life of the option, this riskless portfolio must also change.

9.8. At the end of two months the value of the option will be either \$4 (if the stock price is \$53) or \$0 (if the stock price is \$48). Consider a portfolio consisting of:

$$+\Delta \quad : \quad \text{shares}$$
$$-1 \quad : \quad \text{option}$$

The value of the portfolio is either 48Δ or $53\Delta - 4$ in two months. If

$$48\Delta = 53\Delta - 4$$

i.e.,

$$\Delta = 0.8$$

the value of the portfolio is certain to be 38.4. For this value of Δ the portfolio is therefore riskless. The current value of the portfolio is:

$$0.8 \times 50 - f$$

where f is the value of the option. Since the portfolio must earn the risk-free rate of interest

$$(0.8 \times 50 - f)e^{0.10 \times 0.16667} = 38.4$$

i.e.,

$$f = 2.23$$

The value of the option is therefore $2.23.

This can also be calculated directly from equations (9.2) and (9.3). $u = 1.06$, $d = 0.96$ so that

$$p = \frac{e^{0.10 \times 0.16667} - 0.96}{1.06 - 0.96} = 0.5681$$

and

$$f = e^{-0.10 \times 0.16667} \times 0.5681 \times 4 = 2.23$$

9.9. At the end of four months the value of the option will be either $5 (if the stock price is $75) or $0 (if the stock price is $85). Consider a portfolio consisting of:

$$-\Delta \quad : \quad \text{shares}$$
$$+1 \quad : \quad \text{option}$$

(Note: The delta, Δ of a put option is negative. We have constructed the portfolio so that it is +1 option and $-\Delta$ shares rather than -1 option and $+\Delta$ shares so that the initial investment is positive.)

The value of the portfolio is either -85Δ or $-75\Delta + 5$ in four months. If

$$-85\Delta = -75\Delta + 5$$

i.e.,

$$\Delta = -0.5$$

the value of the portfolio is certain to be 42.5. For this value of Δ the portfolio is therefore riskless. The current value of the portfolio is:

$$0.5 \times 80 + f$$

where f is the value of the option. Since the portfolio is riskless

$$(0.5 \times 80 + f)e^{0.05 \times 0.3333} = 42.5$$

i.e.,

$$f = 1.80$$

The value of the option is therefore $1.80.

This can also be calculated directly from equations (9.2) and (9.3). $u = 1.0625$, $d = 0.9375$ so that

$$p = \frac{e^{0.05 \times 0.3333} - 0.9375}{1.0625 - 0.9375} = 0.6345$$

$1 - p = 0.3655$ and

$$f = e^{-0.05 \times 0.33333} \times 0.3655 \times 5 = 1.80$$

9.10. At the end of three months the value of the option is either $5 (if the stock price is $35) or $0 (if the stock price is $45).
Consider a portfolio consisting of:

$$-\Delta \quad : \quad \text{shares}$$
$$+1 \quad : \quad \text{option}$$

(Note: The delta, Δ, of a put option is negative. We have constructed the portfolio so that it is $+1$ option and $-\Delta$ shares rather than -1 option and $+\Delta$ shares so that the initial investment is positive.)
The value of the portfolio is either $-35\Delta + 5$ or -45Δ. If:

$$-35\Delta + 5 = -45\Delta$$

i.e.,

$$\Delta = -0.5$$

the value of the portfolio is certain to be 22.5. For this value of Δ the portfolio is therefore riskless. The current value of the portfolio is

$$-40\Delta + f$$

where f is the value of the option. Since the portfolio must earn the risk-free rate of interest

$$(40 \times 0.5 + f) \times 1.02 = 22.5$$

Hence

$$f = 2.06$$

i.e., the value of the option is $2.06.
This can also be calculated using risk-neutral valuation. Suppose that p is the probability of an upward stock price movement in a risk-neutral world. We must have

$$45p + 35(1 - p) = 40 \times 1.02$$

i.e.,

$$10p = 5.8$$

or:

$$p = 0.58$$

The expected value of the option in a risk-neutral world is:

$$0 \times 0.58 + 5 \times 0.42 = 2.10$$

This has a present value of

$$\frac{2.10}{1.02} = 2.06$$

This is consistent with the no-arbitrage answer.

9.11. A tree describing the behavior of the stock price is shown in Figure 9.3. The risk-neutral probability of an up move, p, is given by

$$p = \frac{e^{0.25 \times 0.05} - 0.95}{1.06 - 0.95} = 0.5689$$

There is a payoff from the option of $56.18 - 51 = 5.18$ for the highest final node (which corresponds to two up moves) zero in all other cases. The value of the option is therefore

$$5.18 \times 0.5689^2 \times e^{-0.05 \times 0.5} = 1.635$$

This can also be calculated by working back through the tree. The value of the call option is the lower number at each node in the diagram.

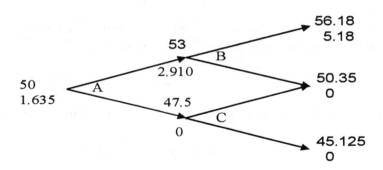

Figure 9.3   Tree for Problem 9.11

9.12. The tree for valuing the put option is shown in Figure 9.4. We get a payoff of $51 - 50.35 = 0.65$ if the middle final node is reached and a payoff of $51 - 45.125 = 5.875$ if the lowest final node is reached. The value of the option is therefore

$$(0.65 \times 2 \times 0.5689 \times 0.4311 + 5.875 \times 0.4311^2)e^{-0.05 \times 0.5} = 1.376$$

This can also be calculated by working back through the tree.
The value of the put plus the stock price is

$$1.376 + 50 = 51.376$$

The value of the call plus the present value of the strike price is

$$1.635 + 51e^{-0.05 \times 0.5} = 51.376$$

This verifies that put–call parity holds

To test whether it worth exercising the option early we compare the value calculated for the option at each node with the payoff from immediate exercise. At node C the payoff from immediate exercise is $51 - 47.5 = 3.5$. Since this is greater than 2.8664, the option should be exercised at this node. The option should not be exercised at either node A or node B.

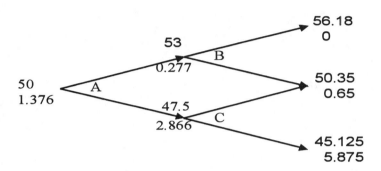

Figure 9.4   Tree for Problem 9.12

9.13. At the end of two months the value of the derivative will be either 529 (if the stock price is 23) or 729 (if the stock price is 27). Consider a portfolio consisting of:

$$+\Delta \quad : \quad \text{shares}$$
$$-1 \quad : \quad \text{derivative}$$

The value of the portfolio is either $27\Delta - 729$ or $23\Delta - 529$ in two months. If

$$27\Delta - 729 = 23\Delta - 529$$

i.e.,

$$\Delta = 50$$

the value of the portfolio is certain to be 621. For this value of Δ the portfolio is therefore riskless. The current value of the portfolio is:

$$50 \times 25 - f$$

where f is the value of the derivative. Since the portfolio must earn the risk-free rate of interest

$$(50 \times 25 - f)e^{0.10 \times 0.16667} = 621$$

i.e.,

$$f = 639.3$$

The value of the option is therefore \$639.3.

This can also be calculated directly from equations (9.2) and (9.3). $u = 1.08$, $d = 0.92$ so that

$$p = \frac{e^{0.10 \times 0.16667} - 0.92}{1.08 - 0.92} = 0.6050$$

and

$$f = e^{-0.10 \times 0.16667}(0.6050 \times 729 + 0.3950 \times 529) = 639.3$$

CHAPTER 10
Model of the Behavior of Stock Prices

10.1. Imagine that you have to forecast the future temperature from a) the current temperature, b) the history of the temperature and c) a knowledge of seasonal averages and seasonal trends. If temperature followed a Markov process, the history of the temperature would be irrelevant.

To answer the second part of the question you might like to consider the following scenario for the first week in May:

(i) Monday to Thursday are warm days; Friday is a very cold day.
(ii) Monday to Friday are all very cold days.

What is your forecast for the weekend? If you are more pessimistic in the case of the second scenario, temperatures do not follow a Markov process.

10.2. The first point to make is that any trading strategy can, just because of good luck, produce above average returns. The key question is whether a trading strategy *consistently* outperforms the market when adjustments are made for risk. It is certainly possible that a trading strategy could do this. However, when enough investors know about the strategy and trade on the basis of the strategy, the profit will disappear.

As an illustration of this, consider a phenomenon known as the small firm effect. Portfolios of stocks in small firms appear to have outperformed portfolios of stocks in large firms when appropriate adjustments are made for risk. Papers were published about this in the early 1980s and mutual funds were set up to take advantage of the phenomenon. There is some evidence that this has resulted in the phenomenon disappearing.

10.3. Suppose that the company's initial cash position is x. The probability distribution of the cash position at the end of one year is

$$\phi(x + 4 \times 0.5, \sqrt{4} \times \sqrt{4}) = \phi(x + 2.0, 4)$$

The probability of a negative cash position at the end of one year is

$$N\left(-\frac{x + 2.0}{4}\right)$$

where $N(x)$ is the cumulative probability that a standardized normal variable (with mean zero and standard deviation 1.0) is less than x. From normal distribution tables

$$N\left(-\frac{x + 2.0}{4}\right) = 0.05$$

when:

$$-\frac{x + 2.0}{4} = -1.6449$$

i.e., when $x = 4.5796$. The initial cash position must therefore be \$4.56 million.

10.4. (a) Suppose that X_1 and X_2 equal a_1 and a_2 initially. After a time period of length T, X_1 has the probability distribution

$$\phi(a_1 + \mu_1 T, \sigma_1\sqrt{T})$$

and X_2 has a probability distribution

$$\phi(a_2 + \mu_2 T, \sigma_2\sqrt{T})$$

From the property of sums of independent normally distributed variables (see footnote 2 in Chapter 10), $X_1 + X_2$ has the probability distribution

$$\phi\left(a_1 + \mu_1 T + a_2 + \mu_2 T, \sqrt{\sigma_1^2 T + \sigma_2^2 T}\right)$$

i.e.,

$$\phi\left[a_1 + a_2 + (\mu_1 + \mu_2)T, \sqrt{(\sigma_1^2 + \sigma_2^2)T}\right]$$

This shows that $X_1 + X_2$ follows a generalized Wiener process with drift rate $\mu_1 + \mu_2$ and variance rate $\sigma_1^2 + \sigma_2^2$.

(b) In this case the change in the value of $X_1 + X_2$ in a short interval of time Δt has the probability distribution:

$$\phi\left[(\mu_1 + \mu_2)\Delta t, \sqrt{(\sigma_1^2 + \sigma_2^2 + 2\rho\sigma_1\sigma_2)\Delta t}\right]$$

If μ_1, μ_2, σ_1, σ_2 and ρ are all constant, arguments similar to those in Section 10.2 show that the change in a longer period of time T is

$$\phi\left[(\mu_1 + \mu_2)T, \sqrt{(\sigma_1^2 + \sigma_2^2 + 2\rho\sigma_1\sigma_2)T}\right]$$

The variable, $X_1 + X_2$, therefore follows a generalized Wiener process with drift rate $\mu_1 + \mu_2$ and variance rate $\sigma_1^2 + \sigma_2^2 + 2\rho\sigma_1\sigma_2$.

10.5. The change in S during the first three years has the probability distribution

$$\phi(2 \times 3, 3 \times \sqrt{3}) = \phi(6, 5.20)$$

The change during the next three years has the probability distribution

$$\phi(3 \times 3, 4 \times \sqrt{3}) = \phi(9, 6.93)$$

The change during the six years is the sum of a variable with probability distribution $\phi(6, 5.20)$ and a variable with probability distribution $\phi(9, 6.93)$. The probability distribution of the change is therefore

$$\phi(6 + 9, \sqrt{5.20^2 + 6.93^2})$$

$$= \phi(15, 8.66)$$

Since the initial value of the variable is 5, the probability distribution of the value of the variable at the end of year six is

$$\phi(20, 8.66)$$

10.6. From Ito's lemma

$$\sigma_G G = \frac{\partial G}{\partial S} \sigma_S S$$

Also the drift of G is

$$\frac{\partial G}{\partial S} \mu S + \frac{\partial G}{\partial t} + \frac{1}{2} \frac{\partial^2 G}{\partial S^2} \sigma^2 S^2$$

where μ is the expected return on the stock. When μ increases by $\lambda \sigma_S$, the drift of G increases by

$$\frac{\partial G}{\partial S} \lambda \sigma_S S$$

or

$$\lambda \sigma_G G$$

The growth rate of G, therefore, increases by $\lambda \sigma_G$.

10.7. Define S_A, μ_A and σ_A as the stock price, expected return and volatility for stock A. Define S_B, μ_B and σ_B as the stock price, expected return and volatility for stock B. Define ΔS_A and ΔS_B as the change in S_A and S_B in time Δt. Since each of the two stocks follows geometric Brownian motion,

$$\Delta S_A = \mu_A S_A \Delta t + \sigma_A S_A \epsilon_A \sqrt{\Delta t}$$

$$\Delta S_B = \mu_B S_B \Delta t + \sigma_B S_B \epsilon_B \sqrt{\Delta t}$$

where ϵ_A and ϵ_B are independent random samples from a normal distribution.

$$\Delta S_A + \Delta S_B = (\mu_A S_A + \mu_B S_B)\Delta t + (\sigma_A S_A \epsilon_A + \sigma_B S_B \epsilon_B)\sqrt{\Delta t}$$

This *cannot* be written as

$$\Delta S_A + \Delta S_B = \mu(S_A + S_B)\Delta t + \sigma(S_A + S_B)\epsilon\sqrt{\Delta t}$$

for any constants μ and σ. (Neither the drift term nor the stochastic term correspond.) Hence the value of the portfolio does not follow geometric Brownian motion.

10.8. In:
$$\Delta S = \mu S \Delta t + \sigma S \epsilon \sqrt{\Delta t}$$

the expected increase in the stock price and the variability of the stock price are constant when both are expressed as a proportion (or as a percentage) of the stock price
In:
$$\Delta S = \mu \Delta t + \sigma \epsilon \sqrt{\Delta t}$$

the expected increase in the stock price and the variability of the stock price are constant in absolute terms. For example if the expected growth rate is \$5 per annum when the stock price is \$25, it is also \$5 per annum when it is \$100. If the standard deviation of weekly stock price movements is \$1 when the price is \$25, it is also \$1 when the price is \$100.
In:
$$\Delta S = \mu S \Delta t + \sigma \epsilon \sqrt{\Delta t}$$

the expected increase in the stock price is a constant proportion of the stock price while the variability is constant in absolute terms.
In:
$$\Delta S = \mu \Delta t + \sigma S \epsilon \sqrt{\Delta t}$$

the expected increase in the stock price is constant in absolute terms while the variability of the proportional stock price change is constant.
The model:
$$\Delta S = \mu S \Delta t + \sigma S \epsilon \sqrt{\Delta t}$$

is the most appropriate one since it is most realistic to assume that the expected *percentage return* and the variability of the *percentage return* in a short interval is constant.

10.9. The drift rate is $a(b - r)$. Thus, when the interest rate is above b the drift rate is negative and, when the interest rate is below b, the drift rate is positive. The interest rate is therefore continually pulled towards the level b. The rate at which it is pulled toward this level is a. A volatility equal to c is superimposed upon the "pull" or the drift.
Suppose $a = 0.4$, $b = 0.1$ and $c = 0.15$ and the current interest rate is 20% per annum. The interest rate is pulled towards the level of 10% per annum. This can be regarded as a long run average. The current drift is -4% per annum so that the expected rate at the end of one year is about 16% per annum. (In fact it is slightly greater than this, because as the interest rate decreases, the "pull" decreases.) Superimposed upon the drift is a volatility of 15% per annum.

10.10. If $G(S, t) = S^n$ then $\partial G/\partial t = 0$, $\partial G/\partial S = nS^{n-1}$, and $\partial^2 G/\partial S^2 = n(n-1)S^{n-2}$. Using Ito's lemma:

$$dG = \left[\mu n G + \frac{1}{2}n(n-1)\sigma^2 G\right]dt + \sigma n G \, dz$$

This shows that $G = S^n$ follows geometric Brownian motion where the expected return is

$$\mu n + \frac{1}{2}n(n-1)\sigma^2$$

and the volatility is $n\sigma$. The stock price S has an expected return of μ and the expected value of S_T is $S_0 e^{\mu T}$. By analogy the expected value of S_T^n is

$$S_0^n e^{[\mu n + \frac{1}{2}n(n-1)\sigma^2]T}$$

10.11. The process followed by B, the bond price, is from Ito's lemma:

$$dB = \left[\frac{\partial B}{\partial x}a(x_0 - x) + \frac{\partial B}{\partial t} + \frac{1}{2}\frac{\partial^2 B}{\partial x^2}s^2 x^2\right]dt + \frac{\partial B}{\partial x}sx dz$$

Since:

$$B = e^{-x(T-t)}$$

the required partial derivatives are

$$\frac{\partial B}{\partial t} = xe^{-x(T-t)} = xB$$

$$\frac{\partial B}{\partial x} = -(T-t)e^{-x(T-t)} = -(T-t)B$$

$$\frac{\partial^2 B}{\partial x^2} = (T-t)^2 e^{-x(T-t)} = (T-t)^2 B$$

Hence:

$$dB = \left[-a(x_0 - x)(T-t) + x + \frac{1}{2}s^2 x^2 (T-t)^2\right]Bdt - sx(T-t)Bdz$$

CHAPTER 11
The Black–Scholes Model

11.1. The Black–Scholes option pricing model assumes that the probability distribution of the stock price in 1 year (or at any other future time) is lognormal. Equivalently, it assumes that the continuously compounded rate of return on the stock is normally distributed.

11.2. The standard deviation of the proportional price change in time Δt is $\sigma\sqrt{\Delta t}$ where σ is the volatility. In this problem $\sigma = 0.3$ and, assuming 252 trading days in one year, $\Delta t = 1/252 = 0.004$ so that $\sigma\sqrt{\Delta t} = 0.3\sqrt{0.004} = 0.019$ or 1.9%.

11.3. The price of an option or other derivative when expressed in terms of the price of the underlying stock is independent of risk preferences. Options therefore have the same value in a risk-neutral world as they do in the real world. We may therefore assume that the world is risk neutral for the purposes of valuing options. This simplifies the analysis. In a risk-neutral world all securities have an expected return equal to risk-free interest rate. Also, in a risk-neutral world, the appropriate discount rate to use for expected future cash flows is the risk-free interest rate.

11.4. In this case $S_0 = 50$, $X = 50$, $r = 0.1$, $\sigma = 0.3$, $T = 0.25$, and

$$d_1 = \frac{\ln(50/50) + (0.1 + 0.09/2)0.25}{0.3\sqrt{0.25}} = 0.2417$$

$$d_2 = d_1 - 0.3\sqrt{0.25} = 0.0917$$

The European put price is

$$50N(-0.0917)e^{-0.1\times0.25} - 50N(-0.2417)$$

$$= 50 \times 0.4634e^{-0.1\times0.25} - 50 \times 0.4045 = 2.37$$

or $2.37.

11.5. In this case we must subtract the present value of the dividend from the stock price before using Black–Scholes. Hence the appropriate value of S_0 is

$$S_0 = 50 - 1.50e^{-0.1667\times0.1} = 48.52$$

As before $X = 50$, $r = 0.1$, $\sigma = 0.3$, and $T = 0.25$. In this case

$$d_1 = \frac{\ln(48.52/50) + (0.1 + 0.09/2)0.25}{0.3\sqrt{0.25}} = 0.0414$$

$$d_2 = d_1 - 0.3\sqrt{0.25} = -0.1086$$

The European put price is

$$50N(0.1086)e^{-0.1 \times 0.25} - 48.52N(-0.0414)$$

$$= 50 \times 0.5432e^{-0.1 \times 0.25} - 48.52 \times 0.4835 = 3.03$$

or \$3.03.

11.6. The implied volatility is the volatility that makes the Black–Scholes price of an option equal to its market price. It is calculated using an iterative procedure.

11.7. In this case $\mu = 0.15$ and $\sigma = 0.25$. From equation (11.7) the probability distribution for the rate of return over a 2-year period with continuous compounding is:

$$\phi\left(0.15 - \frac{0.25^2}{2}, \frac{0.25}{\sqrt{2}}\right)$$

i.e.,

$$\phi(0.11875, 0.1768)$$

The expected value of the return is 11.875% per annum and the standard deviation is 17.68% per annum.

11.8. (a) The required probability is the probability of the stock price being above \$40 in six months' time. Suppose that the stock price in six months is S_T

$$\ln S_T \sim \phi(\ln 38 + (0.16 - \frac{0.35^2}{2})0.5, 0.35\sqrt{0.5})$$

i.e.,

$$\ln S_T \sim \phi(3.687, 0.247)$$

Since $\ln 40 = 3.689$, the required probability is

$$1 - N\left(\frac{3.689 - 3.687}{0.247}\right) = 1 - N(0.008)$$

From normal distribution tables $N(0.008) = 0.5032$ so that the required probability is 0.4968. In general the required probability is $N(d_2)$. (See Problem 11.22).
(b) In this case the required probability is the probability of the stock price being less than \$40 in six months' time. It is

$$1 - 0.4968 = 0.5032$$

11.9. From equation 11.2:

$$\ln S_T \sim \phi[\ln S_0 + (\mu - \frac{\sigma^2}{2})T, \sigma\sqrt{T}]$$

95% confidence intervals for $\ln S_T$ are therefore

$$\ln S_0 + (\mu - \frac{\sigma^2}{2})T - 1.96\sigma\sqrt{T}$$

and

$$\ln S_0 + (\mu - \frac{\sigma^2}{2})T + 1.96\sigma\sqrt{T}$$

95% confidence intervals for S_T are therefore

$$e^{\ln S_0 + (\mu - \sigma^2/2)T - 1.96\sigma\sqrt{T}}$$

and

$$e^{\ln S_0 + (\mu - \sigma^2/2)T + 1.96\sigma\sqrt{T}}$$

i.e.

$$S_0 e^{(\mu - \sigma^2/2)T - 1.96\sigma\sqrt{T}}$$

and

$$S_0 e^{(\mu - \sigma^2/2)T + 1.96\sigma\sqrt{T}}$$

11.10. The statement is misleading in that a certain sum of money, say $1000, when invested for 10 years in the fund would have realized a return (with annual compounding) of less than 20% per annum.

The average of the returns realized in each year is always greater than the return per annum (with annual compounding) realized over 10 years. The first is an arithmetic average of the returns in each year; the second is a geometric average of these returns.

11.11. (a) At time t, the expected value of $\ln S_T$ is, from equation (11.2)

$$\ln S + (\mu - \frac{\sigma^2}{2})(T - t)$$

In a risk-neutral world the expected value of $\ln S_T$ is therefore:

$$\ln S + (r - \frac{\sigma^2}{2})(T - t)$$

Using risk-neutral valuation the value of the security at time t is:

$$e^{-r(T-t)}\left[\ln S + (r - \frac{\sigma^2}{2})(T - t)\right]$$

(b) If:

$$f = e^{-r(T-t)}\left[\ln S + (r - \frac{\sigma^2}{2})(T-t)\right]$$

$$\frac{\partial f}{\partial t} = re^{-r(T-t)}\left[\ln S + (r - \frac{\sigma^2}{2})(T-t)\right] - e^{-r(T-t)}(r - \frac{\sigma^2}{2})$$

$$\frac{\partial f}{\partial S} = \frac{e^{-r(T-t)}}{S}$$

$$\frac{\partial^2 f}{\partial S^2} = -\frac{e^{-r(T-t)}}{S^2}$$

The left-hand side of the Black Scholes differential equation is

$$e^{-r(T-t)}\left[r \ln S + r(r - \frac{\sigma^2}{2})(T-t) - (r - \frac{\sigma^2}{2}) + r - \frac{\sigma^2}{2}\right]$$

$$= re^{-r(T-t)}\left[\ln S + (r - \frac{\sigma^2}{2})(T-t)\right]$$

$$= rf$$

Hence the Black-Scholes equation is satisfied.

11.12. This problem is related to Problem 10.11.

(a)If $G(S,t) = h(t,T)S^n$ then $\partial G/\partial t = h_t S^n$, $\partial G/\partial S = hnS^{n-1}$, and $\partial^2 G/\partial G^2 = hn(n-1)S^{n-2}$ where $h_t = \partial h/\partial t$. Substituting into the Black–Scholes differential equation we obtain

$$h_t + rhn + \frac{1}{2}\sigma^2 hn(n-1) = rh$$

(b)The derivative is worth S^n when $t = T$. The boundary condition for this differential equation is therefore $h(T,T) = 1$

(c)The equation

$$h(t,T) = e^{[0.5\sigma^2 n(n-1)+r(n-1)](T-t)}$$

satisfies the boundary condition since it collapses to $h = 1$ when $t = T$. It can also be shown that it satisfies the differential equation in (a). Alternatively we can solve the differential equation in (a) directly. The differential equation can be written

$$\frac{h_t}{h} = -r(n-1) - \frac{1}{2}\sigma^2 n(n-1)$$

The solution to this is

$$\ln h = [-r(n-1) - \frac{1}{2}\sigma^2 n(n-1)]t + k$$

where k is a constant. Since $\ln h = 0$ when $t = T$ it follows that

$$k = [r(n-1) + \frac{1}{2}\sigma^2 n(n-1)]T$$

so that

$$\ln h = [r(n-1) + \frac{1}{2}\sigma^2 n(n-1)](T-t)$$

or

$$h(t,T) = e^{[0.5\sigma^2 n(n-1)+r(n-1)](T-t)}$$

11.13. In this case $S_0 = 52$, $X = 50$, $r = 0.12$, $\sigma = 0.30$ and $T = 0.25$.

$$d_1 = \frac{\ln(52/50) + (0.12 + 0.3^2/2)0.25}{0.30\sqrt{0.25}} = 0.5365$$

$$d_2 = d_1 - 0.30\sqrt{0.25} = 0.3865$$

The price of the European call is

$$52N(0.5365) - 50e^{-0.12 \times 0.25}N(0.3865)$$

$$= 52 \times 0.7042 - 50e^{-0.03} \times 0.6504$$

$$= 5.06$$

or $5.06.

11.14. In this case $S_0 = 69$, $X = 70$, $r = 0.05$, $\sigma = 0.35$ and $T = 0.5$.

$$d_1 = \frac{\ln(69/70) + (0.05 + 0.35^2/2) \times 0.5}{0.35\sqrt{0.5}} = 0.1666$$

$$d_2 = d_1 - 0.35\sqrt{0.5} = -0.0809$$

The price of the European put is

$$70e^{-0.05 \times 0.5}N(0.0809) - 69N(-0.1666)$$

$$= 70e^{-0.025} \times 0.5323 - 69 \times 0.4338$$

$$= 6.40$$

or $6.40.

11.15. Using the notation of Section 11.12, $D_1 = D_2 = 1$, $X(1 - e^{-r(T-t_2)}) = 65(1 - e^{-0.1 \times 0.1667}) = 1.07$, and $X(1 - e^{-r(t_2-t_1)}) = 65(1 - e^{-0.1 \times 0.25}) = 1.60$. Since

$$D_1 < X(1 - e^{-r(T-t_2)})$$

and

$$D_2 < X(1 - e^{-r(t_2-t_1)})$$

It is never optimal to exercise the call option early. DerivaGem shows that the value of the option is 10.94. The value of the American is, therefore, the same as that of that of the European.

11.16. In the case $c = 2.5$, $S_0 = 15$, $X = 13$, $T = 0.25$, $r = 0.05$. The implied volatility must be calculated using an iterative procedure.

A volatility of 0.2 (or 20% per annum) gives $c = 2.20$. A volatility of 0.3 gives $c = 2.32$. A volatility of 0.4 gives $c = 2.507$. A volatility of 0.39 gives $c = 2.487$. By interpolation the implied volatility is about 0.397 or 39.7% per annum.

11.17. (a) Since $N(x)$ is the cumulative probability that a variable with a standardized normal distribution will be less than x, $N'(x)$ is the probability density function for a standardized normal distribution, that is,

$$N'(x) = \frac{1}{\sqrt{2\pi}}e^{-\frac{x^2}{2}}$$

(b) To prove this note that

$$
\begin{aligned}
\ln S - \frac{d_1^2}{2} &= \ln S - \frac{1}{2}\left[\frac{\ln\frac{S}{X} + (r + \frac{\sigma^2}{2})(T-t)}{\sigma\sqrt{T-t}}\right]^2 \\
&= -\frac{1}{2\sigma^2(T-t)}\left\{-2\sigma^2(T-t)\ln S + \left[\ln\frac{S}{X} + r(T-t)\right]^2\right. \\
&\quad\left. + 2\left[\ln\frac{S}{X} + r(T-t)\right]\frac{\sigma^2}{2}(T-t) + \frac{\sigma^4}{4}(T-t)^2\right\} \\
&= -\frac{1}{2\sigma^2(T-t)}\left\{\left[\ln\frac{S}{X} + r(T-t)\right]^2 + \frac{\sigma^4}{4}(T-t)^2\right. \\
&\quad\left. + \sigma^2(T-t)[\ln S - \ln X + r(T-t) - 2\ln S]\right\} \\
&= -\frac{1}{2\sigma^2(T-t)}\left\{\left[\ln\frac{S}{X} + r(T-t)\right]^2 + \frac{\sigma^4}{4}(T-t)^2\right. \\
&\quad\left. + \sigma^2(T-t)[-\ln S - \ln X + r(T-t)]\right\}
\end{aligned}
$$

Also:

$$\ln X - r(T-t) - \frac{d_2^2}{2} = \ln X - r(T-t) - \frac{1}{2}\left[\frac{\ln\frac{S}{X} + (r - \frac{\sigma^2}{2})(T-t)}{\sigma\sqrt{T-t}}\right]^2$$

$$= -\frac{1}{2\sigma^2(T-t)}\left\{2\sigma^2(T-t)[-\ln X + r(T-t)] + \left[\ln\frac{S}{X} + r(T-t)\right]^2\right.$$

$$\left. - 2\left[\ln\frac{S}{X} + r(T-t)\right]\frac{\sigma^2}{2}(T-t) + \frac{\sigma^4}{4}(T-t)^2\right\}$$

$$= -\frac{1}{2\sigma^2(T-t)}\left\{\left[\ln\frac{S}{X} + r(T-t)\right]^2 + \frac{\sigma^4}{4}(T-t)^2 + \sigma^2(T-t)\right.$$

$$\left. [-\ln S + \ln X - r(T-t) - 2\ln X + 2r(T-t)]\right\}$$

$$= -\frac{1}{2\sigma^2(T-t)}\left\{\left[\ln\frac{S}{X} + r(T-t)\right]^2 + \frac{\sigma^4}{4}(T-t)^2\right.$$

$$\left. + \sigma^2(T-t)[-\ln S - \ln X + r(T-t)]\right\}$$

This rather tedious algebra shows that

$$\ln S - \frac{d_1^2}{2} = \ln X - r(T-t) - \frac{d_2^2}{2}$$

Hence

$$e^{\ln S - d_1^2/2} = e^{\ln X - r(T-t) - d_2^2/2}$$

and

$$Se^{-d_1^2/2} = Xe^{-r(T-t)}e^{-d_2^2/2}$$

It follows that

$$SN'(d_1) = Xe^{-r(T-t)}N'(d_2)$$

(c)

$$d_1 = \frac{\ln\frac{S}{X} + (r + \frac{\sigma^2}{2})(T-t)}{\sigma\sqrt{T-t}}$$

$$= \frac{\ln S - \ln X + (r + \frac{\sigma^2}{2})(T-t)}{\sigma\sqrt{T-t}}$$

Hence

$$\frac{\partial d_1}{\partial S} = \frac{1}{S\sigma\sqrt{T-t}}$$

Similarly

$$d_2 = \frac{\ln S - \ln X + (r - \frac{\sigma^2}{2})(T - t)}{\sigma\sqrt{T - t}}$$

and

$$\frac{\partial d_2}{\partial S} = \frac{1}{S\sigma\sqrt{T - t}}$$

Therefore:

$$\frac{\partial d_1}{\partial S} = \frac{\partial d_2}{\partial S}$$

(d)

$$c = SN(d_1) - Xe^{-r(T-t)}N(d_2)$$

$$\frac{\partial c}{\partial t} = SN'(d_1)\frac{\partial d_1}{\partial t} - rXe^{-r(T-t)}N(d_2) - Xe^{-r(T-t)}N'(d_2)\frac{\partial d_2}{\partial t}$$

From (b):

$$SN'(d_1) = Xe^{-r(T-t)}N'(d_2)$$

Hence

$$\frac{\partial c}{\partial t} = -rXe^{-r(T-t)}N(d_2) + SN'(d_1)\left(\frac{\partial d_1}{\partial t} - \frac{\partial d_2}{\partial t}\right)$$

Since

$$d_1 - d_2 = \sigma\sqrt{T - t}$$

$$\frac{\partial d_1}{\partial t} - \frac{\partial d_2}{\partial t} = \frac{\partial}{\partial t}(\sigma\sqrt{T - t})$$

$$= -\frac{\sigma}{2\sqrt{T - t}}$$

Hence

$$\frac{\partial c}{\partial t} = -rXe^{-r(T-t)}N(d_2) - SN'(d_1)\frac{\sigma}{2\sqrt{T - t}}$$

(e) From differentiating the Black–Scholes formula for a call price we obtain

$$\frac{\partial c}{\partial S} = N(d_1) + SN'(d_1)\frac{\partial d_1}{\partial S} - Xe^{-r(T-t)}N'(d_2)\frac{\partial d_2}{dS}$$

From the results in (b) and (c) it follows that

$$\frac{\partial c}{\partial S} = N(d_1)$$

(f) Differentiating the result in (e) and using the result in (c), we obtain

$$\frac{\partial^2 c}{\partial S^2} = N'(d_1)\frac{\partial d_1}{\partial S}$$

$$= N'(d_1)\frac{1}{S\sigma\sqrt{T - t}}$$

69

From the results in d) and e)

$$\frac{\partial c}{\partial t} + rS\frac{\partial c}{\partial S} + \frac{1}{2}\sigma^2 S^2 \frac{\partial^2 c}{\partial S^2} = -rXe^{-r(T-t)}N(d_2) - SN'(d_1)\frac{\sigma}{2\sqrt{T-t}}$$

$$+ rSN(d_1) + \frac{1}{2}\sigma^2 S^2 N'(d_1)\frac{1}{S\sigma\sqrt{T-t}}$$

$$= r[SN(d_1) - Xe^{-r(T-t)}N(d_2)]$$

$$= rc$$

This shows that the Black–Scholes formula for a call option does indeed satisfy the Black–Scholes differential equation

11.18. From the Black–Scholes equations

$$p + S_0 = Xe^{-rT}N(-d_2) - S_0N(-d_1) + S_0$$

Because $1 - N(-d_1) = N(d_1)$ this is

$$Xe^{-rT}N(-d_2) + S_0N(d_1)$$

Also:

$$c + Xe^{-rT} = S_0N(d_1) - Xe^{-rT}N(d_2) + Xe^{-rT}$$

Because $1 - N(d_2) = N(-d_2)$, this is also

$$Xe^{-rT}N(-d_2) + S_0N(d_1)$$

The Black–Scholes equations are therefore consistent with put–call parity.

11.19. Using DerivaGem we obtain the following table of implied volatilities

Strike Price ($)	Maturity (months)		
	3	6	12
45	37.78	34.99	34.02
50	34.15	32.78	32.03
55	31.98	30.77	30.45

The option prices are not exactly consistent with Black–Scholes. If they were, the implied volatilities would be all the same. We usually find in practice that low strike price options on a stock have significantly higher implied volatilities than high strike price options on the same stock. This phenomenon is discussed in Chapter 17.

11.20. Black's approach in effect assumes that the holder of option must decide at time zero whether it is a European option maturing at time t_n (the final ex-dividend date) or a European option maturing at time T. In fact the holder of the option has more flexibility than this. The holder can choose to exercise at time t_n if the stock price at that time is above some level but not otherwise. Furthermore, if the option is not exercised at time t_n, it can still be exercised at time T.

It appears that Black's approach understates the true option value. This is because the holder of the option has more alternative strategies for deciding when to exercise the option than the two alternatives implicitly assumed by the approach. These alternatives add value to the option. In fact Black's approach sometimes gives a higher value than the approach in Appendix 11A. This is because Appendix 11A applies the volatility to the stock price less the present value of the dividend whereas Black's approach when considering exercise just prior to the dividend date applies the volatility to the stock price itself. Thus part of the Black calculation assumes more stock price variability than Roll–Geske–Whaley. This issue is also discussed in Example 11.8.

11.21. With the notation in the text

$$D_1 = D_2 = 1, \quad t_1 = 0.25, \quad t_2 = 0.50, \quad T = 0.6667, \quad r = 0.1 \quad \text{and} \quad X = 65$$

$$X\left[1 - e^{-r(T-t_2)}\right] = 65(1 - e^{-0.1 \times 0.1667}) = 1.07$$

Hence

$$D_2 < X\left[1 - e^{-r(T-t_2)}\right]$$

Also:

$$X\left[1 - e^{-r(t_2-t_1)}\right] = 65(1 - e^{-0.1 \times 0.25}) = 1.60$$

Hence:

$$D_1 < X\left[1 - e^{-r(t_2-t_1)}\right]$$

It follows from the conditions established in Section 11.12 that the option should never be exercised early.

The present value of the dividends is

$$e^{-0.25 \times 0.1} + e^{-0.50 \times 0.1} = 1.9265$$

The option can be valued using the European pricing formula with:

$$S_0 = 68.0735, \quad X = 65, \quad \sigma = 0.32, \quad r = 0.1, \quad T = 0.6667$$

$$d_1 = \frac{\ln(68.0735/65) + (0.1 + 0.32^2/2)0.6667}{0.32\sqrt{0.6667}} = 0.5626$$

$$d_2 = d_1 - 0.32\sqrt{0.6667} = 0.3013$$

$$N(d_1) = 0.7131, \quad N(d_2) = 0.6184$$

and the call price is

$$68.0735 \times 0.7131 - 65e^{-0.1 \times 0.6667} \times 0.6184 = 10.94$$

or $10.94.

11.22. The probability that the call option will be exercised is the probability that $S_T > X$ where S_T is the stock price at time T. In a risk neutral world

$$\ln S_T \sim \phi[\ln S_0 + (r - \sigma^2/2)T, \sigma\sqrt{T}]$$

The probability that $S_T > X$ is the same as the probability that $\ln S_T > \ln X$. This is

$$1 - N\left[\frac{\ln X - \ln S_0 - (r - \sigma^2/2)T}{\sigma\sqrt{T}}\right]$$

$$= N\left[\frac{\ln(S_0/X) + (r - \sigma^2/2)T}{\sigma\sqrt{T}}\right]$$

$$= N(d_2)$$

The expected value at time T in a risk neutral world of a derivative security which pays off $100 when $S_T > X$ is therefore

$$100N(d_2)$$

From risk neutral valuation the value of the security at time t is

$$100e^{-rT}N(d_2)$$

11.23. If $f = S^{-2r/\sigma^2}$ then

$$\frac{\partial f}{\partial S} = -\frac{2r}{\sigma^2}S^{-2r/\sigma^2 - 1}$$

$$\frac{\partial^2 f}{\partial S^2} = \left(\frac{2r}{\sigma^2}\right)\left(\frac{2r}{\sigma^2} + 1\right)S^{-2r/\sigma^2 - 2}$$

$$\frac{\partial f}{\partial t} = 0$$

$$\frac{\partial f}{\partial t} + rS\frac{\partial f}{\partial S} + \frac{1}{2}\sigma^2 S^2\frac{\partial^2 f}{\partial S^2} = rS^{-2r/\sigma^2} = rf$$

This shows that the Black–Scholes equation is satisfied. S^{-2r/σ^2} could therefore be the price of a traded security.

CHAPTER 12
Options on Stock Indices, Currencies, and Futures

12.1. When the S&P 100 goes down to 480, the value of the portfolio can be expected to be $10 \times (480/500) = \$9.6$ million. (This assumes that the dividend yield on the portfolio equals the dividend yield on the index.) Buying put options on $10,000,000/500 = 20,000$ times the index with a strike of 480 therefore provides protection against a drop in the value of the portfolio below \$9.6 million. Since each contract is on 100 times the index a total of 200 contracts would be required.

12.2. A stock index is analogous to a stock paying a continuous dividend yield, the dividend yield being the dividend yield on the index. A currency is analogous to a stock paying a continuous dividend yield, the dividend yield being the foreign risk-free interest rate. A futures contract is analogous to a stock paying a continuous dividend yield, the dividend yield being the domestic risk-free interest rate.

12.3. The lower bound is given by Equation 12.1 as
$$300e^{-0.03 \times 0.5} - 290e^{-0.08 \times 0.5} = 16.90$$

12.4. The tree of exchange-rate movements is shown in Figure 12.1. In this case $u = 1.02$ and $d = 0.98$. The probability of an up movement is
$$p = \frac{e^{(0.06-0.08) \times 0.08333} - 0.98}{1.02 - 0.98} = 0.4584$$

The tree shows that the value of an option to purchase one unit of the currency is \$0.0067.

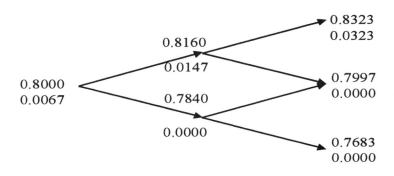

Figure 12.1   Tree for Problem 12.4

73

12.5. A call option on yen gives the holder the right to buy yen in the spot market at an exchange rate equal to the strike price. A call option on yen futures gives the holder the right to receive the amount by which the futures price exceeds the strike price. If the yen futures option is exercised, the holder also obtains a long position in the yen futures contract.

12.6. A company that knows it is due to receive a foreign currency at a certain time in the future can buy a put option. This guarantees that the price at which the currency will be sold will be at or above a certain level. A company that knows it is due to pay a foreign currency a certain time in the future can buy a call option. This guarantees that the price at which the currency will be purchased will be at or below a certain level.

12.7. In this case, $S_0 = 250$, $X = 250$, $r = 0.10$, $\sigma = 0.18$, $T = 0.25$, $q = 0.03$ and

$$d_1 = \frac{\ln(250/250) + (0.10 - 0.03 + 0.18^2/2)0.25}{0.18\sqrt{0.25}} = 0.2394$$

$$d_2 = d_1 - 0.18\sqrt{0.25} = 0.1494$$

and the call price is

$$250N(0.2394)e^{-0.03 \times 0.25} - 250N(0.1494)e^{-0.10 \times 0.25}$$

$$= 250 \times 0.5946e^{-0.03 \times 0.25} - 250 \times 0.5594e^{-0.10 \times 0.25}$$

$$= 12.14$$

12.8. The American futures option is worth more than the corresponding American option on the underlying asset when the futures price is greater than the spot price prior to the maturity of the futures contract. This is the case when the cost of carry net of the convenience yield is positive.

12.9. In this case $S_0 = 0.52$, $X = 0.50$, $r = 0.04$, $r_f = 0.08$, $\sigma = 0.12$, $T = 0.6667$, and

$$d_1 = \frac{\ln(0.52/0.50) + (0.04 - 0.08 + 0.12^2/2)0.6667}{0.12\sqrt{0.6667}} = 0.1771$$

$$d_2 = d_1 - 0.12\sqrt{0.6667} = 0.0791$$

and the put price is

$$0.50N(-0.0791)e^{-0.04 \times 0.6667} - 0.52N(-0.1771)e^{-0.08 \times 0.6667}$$

$$= 0.50 \times 0.4685e^{-0.04 \times 0.6667} - 0.52 \times 0.4297e^{-0.08 \times 0.6667}$$

$$= 0.0162$$

12.10. The main reason is that a bond futures contract is a more liquid instrument than a bond. The price of a Treasury bond futures contract is known immediately from trading on CBOT. The price of a bond can be obtained only by contacting dealers.

12.11. A futures price behaves like a stock paying a continuous dividend yield at the risk-free interest rate.

12.12. In this case $u = 1.12$ and $d = 0.92$. The probability of an up movement in a risk-neutral world is

$$\frac{1 - 0.92}{1.12 - 0.92} = 0.4$$

From risk-neutral valuation, the value of the call is

$$e^{-0.06 \times 0.5}(0.4 \times 6 + 0.6 \times 0) = 2.33$$

12.13. In this case $F_0 = 19$, $X = 20$, $r = 0.12$, $\sigma = 0.20$, and $T = 0.4167$. The value of the European put futures option is

$$20N(-d_2)e^{-0.12 \times 0.4167} - 19N(-d_1)e^{-0.12 \times 0.4167}$$

where

$$d_1 = \frac{\ln(19/20) + (0.04/2)0.4167}{0.2\sqrt{0.4167}} = -0.3327$$

$$d_2 = d_1 - 0.2\sqrt{0.4167} = -0.4618$$

This is

$$e^{-0.12 \times 0.4167}[20N(0.4618) - 19N(0.3327)]$$

$$= e^{-0.12 \times 0.4167}(20 \times 0.6778 - 19 \times 0.6303)$$

$$= 1.50$$

or $1.50.

12.14. A total return index behaves like a stock paying no dividends. In a risk-neutral world it can be expected to grow on average at the risk-free rate. Forward contracts and options on total return indices should be valued in the same way as forward contracts and options on non-dividend-paying stocks.

12.15. In this case $S_0 = 696$, $X = 700$, $r = 0.07$, $\sigma = 0.3$, $T = 0.25$ and $q = 0.04$. The option can be valued using equation (12.5).

$$d_1 = \frac{\ln(696/700) + (0.07 - 0.04 + 0.09/2) \times 0.25}{0.3\sqrt{0.25}} = 0.0868$$

$$d_2 = d_1 - 0.3\sqrt{0.25} = -0.0632$$

and
$$N(-d_1) = 0.4654, \quad N(-d_2) = 0.5252$$

The value of the put, p, is given by:

$$p = 700e^{-0.07 \times 0.25} \times 0.5252 - 696e^{-0.04 \times 0.25} \times 0.4654 = 40.6$$

i.e., it is $40.6.

12.16. The put–call parity relationship for European currency options is

$$c + Xe^{-rT} = p + Se^{-r_f T}$$

To prove this result, the two portfolios to consider are:

Portfolio A: one call option plus one discount bond which will be worth X at time T

Portfolio B: one put option plus $e^{-r_f T}$ of foreign currency invested at the foreign risk-free interest rate.

Both portfolios are worth $\max(S_T, X)$ at time T. They must therefore be worth the same today. The result follows.

12.17. Lower bound for European option is

$$S_0 e^{-r_f T} - Xe^{-rT} = 1.5e^{-0.09 \times 0.5} - 1.4e^{-0.05 \times 0.5} = 0.069$$

Lower bound for American option is

$$S_0 - X = 0.10$$

12.18. In this case $S_0 = 250$, $q = 0.04$, $r = 0.06$, $T = 0.25$, $X = 245$, and $c = 10$. Using put–call parity

$$c + Xe^{-rT} = p + S_0 e^{-qT}$$

or

$$p = c + Xe^{-rT} - S_0 e^{-qT}$$

Substituting:
$$p = 10 + 245e^{-0.25 \times 0.06} - 250e^{-0.25 \times 0.04} = 3.84$$

The put price is 3.84.

12.19. Following the hint, we first consider

Portfolio A: A European call option plus an amount X invested at the risk-free rate

Portfolio B: An American put option plus e^{-qT} of stock with dividends being reinvested in the stock.

76

Portfolio A is worth $c + X$ while portfolio B is worth $P + S_0 e^{-qT}$. If the put option is exercised at time $\tau (0 \leq \tau \leq T)$, portfolio B becomes:

$$X - S_\tau + S_\tau e^{-q(T-\tau)} \leq X$$

where S_τ is the stock price at time τ. Portfolio A is worth

$$c + X e^{r\tau} > X$$

Hence portfolio A is worth more than portfolio B. If both portfolios are held to maturity (time T), portfolio A is worth

$$\max(S_T - X, 0) + X e^{rT}$$
$$= \max(S_T, X) + X[e^{rT} - 1]$$

Portfolio B is worth $\max(S_T, X)$. Hence portfolio A is worth more than portfolio B. Since portfolio A is worth more than portfolio B in all circumstances so that

$$P + S_0 e^{-qT} < c + X$$

Since $c \leq C$:
$$P + S_0 e^{-qT} < C + X$$

or
$$S_0 e^{-qT} - X < C - P$$

This proves the first part of the inequality.

For the second part consider:

> *Portfolio C*: An American call option plus an amount $X e^{-rT}$ invested at the risk-free rate
>
> *Portfolio D*: A European put option plus one stock with dividends being reinvested in the stock.

Portfolio C is worth $C + X e^{-rT}$ while portfolio D is worth $p + S_0$. If the call option is exercised at time $\tau (0 \leq \tau < T)$ portfolio C becomes:

$$S_\tau - X + X e^{-r(T-\tau)} < S_\tau$$

while portfolio D is worth
$$p + S_\tau e^{q(\tau - t)} > S_\tau$$

Hence portfolio D is worth more than portfolio C. If both portfolios are held to maturity (time T), portfolio C is worth $\max(S_T, X)$ while portfolio D is worth

$$\max(X - S_T, 0) + S_T e^{qT}$$
$$= \max(S_T, X) + S_T[e^{qT} - 1]$$

Hence portfolio D is worth more than portfolio C.

Since portfolio D is worth more than portfolio C in all circumstances:

$$C + Xe^{-rT} < p + S_0$$

Since $p < P$:

$$C + Xe^{-rT} < P + S_0$$

or

$$C - P < S_0 - Xe^{-rT}$$

This proves the second part of the inequality. Hence:

$$S_0 e^{-qT} - X < C - P < S_0 - Xe^{-rT}$$

12.20. In this case we consider

Portfolio A: A European call option on futures plus an amount X invested at the risk-free interest rate

Portfolio B: An American put option on futures plus an amount $F_0 e^{-rT}$ invested at the risk-free interest rate plus a futures contract maturing at time T.

Following the arguments in Chapter 3 we will treat all futures contracts as forward contracts. Portfolio A is worth $c + X$ while portfolio B is worth $P + F_0 e^{-rT}$. If the put option is exercised at time $\tau (0 \le \tau \le T)$, portfolio B becomes:

$$X - F_\tau + F_0 e^{-rT} + F_\tau - F_0$$
$$= X + F_0 e^{-rT} - F_0 < X$$

where F_τ is the futures price at time τ. Portfolio A is worth

$$c + Xe^{r\tau} > X$$

Hence portfolio A is worth more than portfolio B. If both portfolios are held to maturity (time T) portfolio A is worth

$$\max(F_T - X, 0) + Xe^{rT}$$
$$= \max(F_T, X) + X[e^{rT} - 1]$$

Portfolio B is worth

$$\max(X - F_T, 0) + F_0 + F_T - F_0 = \max(F_T, X)$$

Hence portfolio A is worth more than portfolio B.
Since portfolio A is worth more than portfolio B in all circumstances:

$$P + F_0 e^{-r(T-t)} < c + X$$

Since $c < C$ it follows that

$$P + F_0 e^{-rT} < C + X$$

or

$$F_0 e^{-rT} - X < C - P$$

This proves the first part of the inequality.

For the second part of the inequality consider:

   Portfolio C: An American call futures option plus an amount Xe^{-rT} invested at the risk-free interest rate

   Portfolio D: A European put futures option plus an amount F_0 invested at the risk-free interest rate plus a futures contract.

Portfolio C is worth $C + Xe^{-rT}$ while portfolio D is worth $p + F_0$. If the call option is exercised at time $\tau (0 \leq \tau < T)$ portfolio C becomes:

$$F_\tau - X + Xe^{-r(T-\tau)} < F_\tau$$

while portfolio D is worth

$$p + F_0 e^{r\tau} + F_\tau - F_0$$
$$= p + F_0[e^{r\tau} - 1] + F_\tau > F_\tau$$

Hence portfolio D is worth more than portfolio C. If both portfolios are held to maturity (time T), portfolio C is worth $\max(F_T, X)$ while portfolio D is worth

$$\max(X - F_T, 0) + F_0 e^{rT} + F_T - F_0$$
$$= \max(X, F_T) + F_0[e^{rT} - 1]$$
$$> \max(X, F_T)$$

Hence portfolio D is worth more than portfolio C.

Since portfolio D is worth more than portfolio C in all circumstances

$$C + Xe^{-rT} < p + F_0$$

Since $p < P$ it follows that

$$C + Xe^{-rT} < P + F_0$$

or

$$C - P < F_0 - Xe^{-rT}$$

This proves the second part of the inequality. The result:

$$F_0 e^{-rT} - X < C - P < F_0 - Xe^{-rT}$$

has therefore been proved.

12.21. The risk-neutral process for the price of currency A in terms of the price of currency B is

$$dS = (r_B - r_A)Sdt + \sigma Sdz$$

The price of currency B expressed in terms of currency A is $1/S$. Define

$$G = \frac{1}{S}$$

then:

$$\frac{\partial G}{\partial t} = 0; \quad \frac{\partial G}{\partial S} = -\frac{1}{S^2}; \quad \frac{\partial^2 G}{\partial S^2} = \frac{2}{S^3}$$

Applying Ito's lemma:

$$
\begin{aligned}
dG &= \left(-\frac{1}{S^2}\mu S + \frac{1}{2}\frac{2}{S^3}\sigma^2 S^2 \right) dt - \frac{1}{S^2}\sigma S dz \\
&= \frac{1}{S}\left(-\mu + \sigma^2 \right) dt - \frac{1}{S}\sigma dz \\
&= (-\mu + \sigma^2)G dt - \sigma G dz
\end{aligned}
$$

We can define a process dz^* by:

$$dz^* = -dz$$

This is also a Wiener process and:

$$dG = (r_A - r_B + \sigma^2)G dt + \sigma G dz^*$$

This shows that $G = 1/S$ follows geometric Brownian motion. The expected growth rate might be expected to be $r_A - r_B$ rather than $r_A - r_B + \sigma^2$. This result is sometimes referred to as Siegel's paradox and is discussed in Chapter 19.

12.22. The volatility of a stock index can be expected to be less than the volatility of a typical stock. This is because some risk (i.e., return uncertainty) is diversified away when a portfolio of stocks is created. In capital asset pricing model terminology, there exists systematic and unsystematic risk in the returns from an individual stock. However, in a stock index, unsystematic risk has been largely diversified away and only the systematic risk contributes to volatility.

12.23. The cost of portfolio insurance increases as the beta of the portfolio increases. This is because portfolio insurance involves the purchase of a put option on an index. As beta increases, the volatility of the index increases and the cost of the put option also increases.

12.24. If the value of the portfolio mirrors the value of the index, the index can be expected to have dropped by 10% when the value of the portfolio drops by 10%. Hence when the value of the portfolio drops to $54 million the value of the index can be expected to be 1080. This indicates that put options with an exercise price of 1080 should be purchased. The options should be on:

$$\frac{60,000,000}{1200} = \$50,000$$

times the index. Each option contract is for $100 times the index. Hence 500 contracts should be purchased.

12.25. When the value of the portfolio falls to $54 million the holder of the portfolio makes a capital loss of 10%. After dividends are taken into account the loss is 7% during the year. This is 12% below the risk-free interest rate. According to the capital asset pricing model:

$$\text{Excess expected return of portfolio above riskless interest rate} = \beta \times \text{Excess expected return of market above riskless interest rate}$$

Therefore, when the portfolio provides a return 12% below the risk-free interest rate, the market's expected return is 6% below the risk-free interest rate. As the index can be assumed to have a beta of 1.0, this is also the excess expected return (including dividends) from the index. The expected return from the index is therefore -1% per annum. Since the index provides a 3% per annum dividend yield, the expected movement in the index is -4%. Thus when the portfolio's value is $54 million the expected value of the index $0.96 \times 1200 = 1152$. Hence European put options should be purchased with an exercise price of 1152. Their maturity date should be in one year.

The number of options required is twice the number required in Problem 12.24. This is because we wish to protect a portfolio which is twice as sensitive to changes in market conditions as the portfolio in Problem 12.24. Hence options on $100,000 (or 1,000 contracts) should be purchased. To check that the answer is correct consider what happens when the value of the portfolio declines by 20% to $48 million. The return including dividends is -17%. This is 22% less than the risk-free interest rate. The index can be expected to provide a return (including dividends) which is 11% less than the risk-free interest rate, i.e. a return of -6%. The index can therefore be expected to drop by 9% to 1092. The payoff from the put options is $(1152 - 1092) \times 100,000 = \$6$ million. This is exactly what is required to restore the value of the portfolio to $54 million.

12.26. Consider the following two portfolios
  Portfolio A: one call option plus one zero-coupon bond which will be worth X at time T
  Portfolio B: one put option plus e^{-qT} of the stock portfolio underlying the index
We assume that the dividends on the stock portfolio are reinvested in the stock portfolio. This means that at maturity portfolio B equals one put option plus one unit of the stock portfolio underlying the index. It is worth $\max(S_T, X)$. Similarly portfolio

81

A is worth $\max(S_T, X)$. As the two portfolios are worth the same at time T, they must be worth the same today.
Hence

$$c + Xe^{-rT} = p + S_0 e^{-qT}$$

12.27. An amount $(400 - 380) \times 100 = \$2,000$ is added to your margin account and you acquire a short futures position giving you the right to sell 100 ounces of gold in October. This position is marked to market at the end of each day in the usual way until you choose to close it out.

12.28. In this case an amount $(0.75 - 0.70) \times 40,000 = \$2,000$ is subtracted from your margin account and you acquire a short position in a live cattle futures contract to sell 40,000 pounds of cattle in April. This position is marked to marked at the end of each day in the usual way until you choose to close it out.

12.29. Lower bound if option is European is

$$(F_0 - X)e^{-rT} = (47 - 40)e^{-0.1 \times 0.1667} = 6.88$$

Lower bound if option is American is

$$F_0 - X = 7$$

12.30. Lower bound if option is European is

$$(X - F_0)e^{-rT} = (50 - 47)e^{-0.1 \times 0.3333} = 2.90$$

Lower bound if option is American is

$$X - F_0 = 3$$

12.31 In this case the risk-neutral probability of an up move is

$$\frac{1 - 0.9}{1.1 - 0.9} = 0.5$$

In the tree shown in Figure 12.2 the middle number at each node is the price of the European option and the lower number is the price of the American option. The tree shows that the price of both the European and the American option is 3.0265. The American option should never be exercised early.

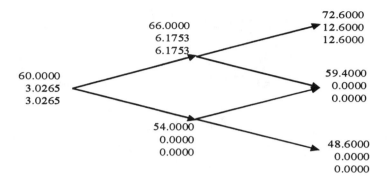

Figure 12.2 Tree to evaluate European and American call options in Problem 12.31.

12.32. In this case the risk-neutral probability of an up move is

$$\frac{1 - 0.9}{1.1 - 0.9} = 0.5$$

The tree in Figure 12.3 shows that the price of the European option is 3.0265 while the price of the American option is 3.0847.

Using the result in the previous problem

$$c + Xe^{-rT} = 3.0265 + 60e^{-0.04} = 60.6739$$

From this problem

$$p + F_0e^{-rT} = 3.0265 + 60e^{-0.04} = 60.6739$$

This verifies that the put–call parity relationship in equation (12.13) holds for the European option prices. For the American option prices we have:

$$C - P = -0.0582; \qquad F_0e^{-rT} - X = -2.353; \qquad F_0 - Xe^{-rT} = 2.353$$

The put–call inequalities for American options are therefore satisfied

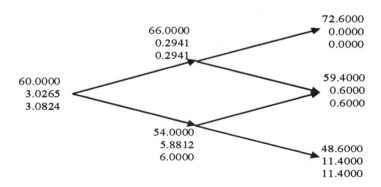

Figure 12.3 Tree to evaluate European and American call options in Problem 12.32.

12.33. In this case $F_0 = 25$, $X = 26$, $\sigma = 0.3$, $r = 0.1$, $T = 0.75$

$$d_1 = \frac{\ln(F_0/X) + \sigma^2 T/2}{\sigma\sqrt{T}} = -0.0211$$

$$d_2 = \frac{\ln(F_0/X) - \sigma^2 T/2}{\sigma\sqrt{T}} = -0.2809$$

$$c = e^{-0.075}[25N(-0.0211) - 26N(-0.2809)]$$

$$= e^{-0.075}[25 \times 0.4916 - 26 \times 0.3894] = 2.01$$

12.34. In this case $F_0 = 70$, $X = 65$, $\sigma = 0.2$, $r = 0.06$, $T = 0.4167$

$$d_1 = \frac{\ln(F_0/X) + \sigma^2 T/2}{\sigma\sqrt{T}} = 0.6386$$

$$d_2 = \frac{\ln(F_0/X) - \sigma^2 T/2}{\sigma\sqrt{T}} = 0.5095$$

$$p = e^{-0.025}[65N(-0.5095) - 70N(-0.6386)]$$

$$= e^{-0.025}[65 \times 0.3052 - 70 \times 0.2615] = 1.495$$

12.35. In this case

$$c + Xe^{-rT} = 2 + 34e^{-0.1 \times 1} = 30.76$$

$$p + F_0 e^{-rT} = 2 + 35e^{-0.1 \times 1} = 31.67$$

Put-call parity shows that the put is overpriced relative to the call. We should buy one call, short one put and short $e^{-0.1} = 0.90$ of the stock.

12.36. The put price is

$$e^{-rT}[XN(-d_1) - F_0 N(-d_2)]$$

Since $N(-x) = 1 - N(x)$ for all x the put price can also be written

$$e^{-rT}[X - XN(d_1) - F_0 + FN(d_2)]$$

Since $F = X$ this is the same as the call price:

$$e^{-rT}[F_0 N(d_1) - XN(d_2)]$$

12.37. From the result at the end of Section 12.5, $C - P$ must lie between

$$30 - 28e^{-0.05 \times 0.25} = 2.35$$

and
$$28 - 30e^{-0.05 \times 0.25} = -1.63$$

Since $C = 4$ we must have
$$1.65 < P < 5.63$$

12.38. A bull spread pays off \$30 at maturity if the asset price is greater than \$330 at maturity. The CAP pays off \$30 if the asset price ever rises above \$330. The payoff from the CAP is always at least as great as that from the the bull spread. The CAP is therefore worth more.

12.39. There is no way of doing this. A natural idea is to create an option to exchange X euros for one yen from an option to exchange Y dollars for 1 yen and an option to exchange X euros for Y dollars. The problem with this is that it assumes that either both options are exercised or that neither option is exercised. There are always some circumstances where the first option is in-the-money at expiration while the second is not and vice versa.

CHAPTER 13
The Greek Letters

13.1. A delta of 0.7 means that, when the price of the stock increases by a small amount, the price of the option increases by 70% of this amount. Similarly, when the price of the stock decreases by a small amount, the price of the option decreases by 70% of this amount. A short position in 1,000 options has a delta of -700 and can be made delta neutral with the purchase of 700 shares.

13.2. In this case $S_0 = X$, $r = 0.1$, $\sigma = 0.25$, and $T = 0.5$. Also,

$$d_1 = \frac{\ln(S_0/X) + (0.1 + 0.25^2/2)0.5}{0.25\sqrt{0.5}} = 0.3712$$

The delta of the option is $N(d_1)$ or 0.64.

13.3. A theta of -0.1 means that if Δt years pass with no change in either the stock price or its volatility, the value of the option declines by $0.1\Delta t$. If a trader feels that neither the stock price nor its implied volatility will change, he or she should write an option with as high a theta as possible. Relatively short-life at-the-money options have the highest theta.

13.4. The gamma of an option position is the rate of change of the delta of the position with respect to the asset price. For example, a gamma of 0.1 would indicate that when the asset price increases by a certain small amount delta increases by 0.1 of this amount. When the gamma of an option writer's position is large and negative and the delta is zero, the option writer will lose significant amounts of money if there is a large movement (either an increase or a decrease) in the asset price.

13.5. To hedge an option position it is necessary to create the opposite option position synthetically. For example, to hedge a long position in a put it is necessary to create a short position in a put synthetically. It follows that the procedure for creating an option position synthetically is the reverse of the procedure for hedging the option position.

13.6. Portfolio insurance involves creating a put option synthetically. It assumes that as soon as a portfolio's value declines by a small amount the portfolio manager's position is rebalanced by either (a) selling part of the portfolio, or (b) selling index futures. On October 19, 1987, the market declined so quickly that the sort of rebalancing anticipated in portfolio insurance schemes could not be accomplished.

13.7. The strategy costs the trader $\$\frac{1}{8}$ each time the stock is bought or sold. The total expected cost of the strategy, in present value terms, must be $4. This means that the expected number of times the stock will be bought or sold is approximately 32. The expected number of times it will be bought is approximately 16 and the expected number of times it will be sold is also approximately 16. The buy and sell transactions can take place at any time during the life of the option. The above numbers are therefore only approximately correct because of the effects of discounting.

13.8. For a non-dividend paying stock, put-call parity gives at a general time t:

$$p + S = c + Xe^{-r(T-t)}$$

(a) Differentiating with respect to S:

$$\frac{\partial p}{\partial S} + 1 = \frac{\partial c}{\partial S}$$

or

$$\frac{\partial p}{\partial S} = \frac{\partial c}{\partial S} - 1$$

This shows that the delta of a European put equals the delta of the corresponding European call less 1.0.
(b) Differentiating with respect to S again

$$\frac{\partial^2 p}{\partial S^2} = \frac{\partial^2 c}{\partial S^2}$$

Hence the gamma of a European put equals the gamma of a European call.
(c) Differentiating the put-call parity relationship with respect to σ

$$\frac{\partial p}{\partial \sigma} = \frac{\partial c}{\partial \sigma}$$

showing that the lambda of a European put equals the lambda of a European call.
(d) Differentiating the put-call parity relationship with respect to T

$$\frac{\partial p}{\partial t} = rXe^{-r(T-t)} + \frac{\partial c}{\partial t}$$

This is in agreement with the thetas of European calls and puts given in Section 13.6 since $N(d_2) = 1 - N(-d_2)$.

13.9. The holding of the stock at any given time must be $N(d_1)$. Hence the stock is bought just after the price has risen and sold just after the price has fallen. (This is the buy high sell low strategy referred to in the text.) In the first scenario the stock is continually bought. In second scenario the stock is bought, sold, bought again, sold again, etc. The final holding is the same in both scenarios. The buy, sell, buy, sell... situation clearly leads to higher costs than the buy, buy, buy... situation. This problem emphasizes one disadvantage of creating options synthetically. Whereas the cost of an option that is purchased is known up front and depends on the forecasted volatility, the cost of an option that is created synthetically is not known up front and depends on the volatility actually encountered.

13.10. The delta of a European futures option is usually defined as the rate of change of the option price with respect to the futures price (not the spot price). It is

$$e^{-rT} N(d_1)$$

In this case $F_0 = 8$, $X = 8$, $r = 0.12$, $\sigma = 0.18$, $T = 0.6667$

$$d_1 = \frac{\ln(8/8) + (0.18^2/2) \times 0.6667}{0.18\sqrt{0.6667}} = 0.0735$$

$N(d_1) = 0.5293$ and the delta of the option is

$$e^{-0.12 \times 0.6667} \times 0.5293 = 0.4886$$

The delta of a short position in 1000 futures options is therefore -488.6.

13.11. In order to answer this problem it is important to distinguish between the rate of change of the price of a derivative security with respect to the futures price and the rate of change of the price of the derivative security with respect to the spot price. The former will be referred to as the futures delta; the latter will be referred to as the spot delta. The futures delta of a nine-month futures contract to buy one ounce of silver is by definition 1.0. Hence, from the answer to problem 13.11, a long position in nine-month futures on 488.6 ounces is necessary to hedge the option position. The spot delta of of a nine-month futures contract is $e^{0.12 \times 0.75} = 1.094$ assuming no storage costs. (This is because silver can be treated in the same way as a non-dividend-paying stock when there are no storage costs.) Hence the spot delta of the option position is $-488.6 \times 1.094 = -534.6$. Thus a long position in 534.6 ounces of silver is necessary to hedge the option position. The spot delta of a one-year silver futures contract to buy one ounce of silver is $e^{0.12} = 1.1275$. Hence a long position in $e^{-0.12} \times 534.6 = 474.1$ ounces of one-year silver futures is necessary to hedge the option position.

13.12. A long position in either a put or a call option has a positive gamma. From Figure 13.8, when gamma is positive the hedger gains from a large change in the stock price and loses from a small change in the stock price. Hence the hedger will fare better in case (b).

13.13. A short position in either a put or a call option has a negative gamma. From Figure 13.8, when gamma is negative the hedger gains from a small change in the stock price and loses from a large change in the stock price. Hence the hedger will fare better in case (a).

13.14. In this case $S_0 = 0.80$, $X = 0.81$, $r = 0.08$, $r_f = 0.05$, $\sigma = 0.15$, $T = 0.5833$

$$d_1 = \frac{\ln(0.80/0.81) + (0.08 - 0.05 + 0.15^2/2) \times 0.5833}{0.15\sqrt{0.5833}} = 0.1016$$

$$d_2 = d_1 - 0.15\sqrt{0.5833} = -0.0130$$

$$N(d_1) = 0.5405; \quad N(d_2) = 0.4998$$

The delta of one call option is $e^{-r_f T}N(d_1) = e^{-0.05 \times 0.5833} \times 0.5405 = 0.5250$.

$$N'(d_1) = \frac{1}{\sqrt{2\pi}}e^{-d_1^2/2} = \frac{1}{\sqrt{2\pi}}e^{-0.00516} = 0.3969$$

so that the gamma of one call option is

$$\frac{N'(d_1)e^{-r_f T}}{S\sigma\sqrt{T}} = \frac{0.3969 \times 0.9713}{0.80 \times 0.15 \times \sqrt{0.5833}} = 4.206$$

The vega of one call option is

$$S_0\sqrt{T}N'(d_1)e^{-r_f T} = 0.80\sqrt{0.5833} \times 0.3969 \times 0.9713 = 0.2355$$

The theta of one call option is

$$-\frac{S_0 N'(d_1)\sigma e^{-r_f T}}{2\sqrt{T}} + r_f S_0 N(d_1)e^{-r_f T} - rXe^{-rT}N(d_2)$$

$$= -\frac{0.8 \times 0.3969 \times 0.15 \times 0.9713}{2\sqrt{0.5833}}$$

$$+ 0.05 \times 0.8 \times 0.5405 \times 0.9713 - 0.08 \times 0.81 \times 0.9544 \times 0.4948$$

$$= -0.0399$$

The rho of one call option is

$$XTe^{-rT}N(d_2)$$

$$= 0.81 \times 0.5833 \times 0.9544 \times 0.4948$$

$$= 0.2231$$

Delta can be interpreted as meaning that, when the spot price increases by a small amount (measured in cents), the value of an option to buy one yen increases by 0.525 times that amount. Gamma can be interpreted as meaning that, when the spot price increases by a small amount (measured in cents), the delta increases by 4.206 times that amount. Vega can be interpreted as meaning that, when the volatility (measured in decimal form) increases by a small amount, the option's value increases by 0.2355 times that amount. Theta can be interpreted as meaning that, when a small amount of time (measured in years) passes, the option's value decreases by 0.0399 times that amount. Finally, rho can be interpreted as meaning that, when the interest rate (measured in decimal form) increases by a small amount the option's value increases by 0.2231 times that amount.

13.15. Assume that S_0, X, r, σ, T, q are the parameters for the over-the-counter option and S_0, X^*, r, σ, T^*, q are the parameters for the traded option. Suppose that d_1 has its usual meaning and is calculated on the basis of the first set of parameters while d_1^* is the value of d_1 calculated on the basis of the second set of parameters. Suppose further that w traded options are held for each over-the-counter option. The gamma of the portfolio is:

$$\alpha \left[\frac{N'(d_1)e^{-qT}}{S_0\sigma\sqrt{T}} + w\frac{N'(d_1^*)e^{-qT^*}}{S_0\sigma\sqrt{T^*}} \right]$$

where α is the number of over-the-counter options held.
Since we require gamma to be zero:

$$w = -\frac{N'(d_1)e^{-q(T-T^*)}}{N'(d_1^*)}\sqrt{\frac{T^*}{T}}$$

The vega of the portfolio is:

$$\alpha \left[S_0\sqrt{T}N'(d_1)e^{-q(T)} + wS_0\sqrt{T^*}N'(d_1^*)e^{-q(T^*)} \right]$$

Since we require vega to be zero:

$$w = -\sqrt{\frac{T}{T^*}}\frac{N'(d_1)e^{-q(T-T^*)}}{N'(d_1^*)}$$

Equating the two expressions for w

$$T^* = T$$

Hence the maturity of the over-the-counter option must equal the maturity of the traded option.

13.16. The fund is worth $300,000 times the value of the index. When the value of the portfolio falls by 5% (to $342 million), the value of the S&P 500 also falls by 5% to 1140. The fund manager therefore requires European put options on the 300,000 times the S&P 500 with exercise price 1020.
(a) $S_0 = 1200$, $X = 1140$, $r = 0.06$, $\sigma = 0.30$, $T = 0.50$ and $q = 0.03$. Hence:

$$d_1 = \frac{\ln(1200/1140) + (0.06 - 0.03 + 0.09/2) \times 0.5}{0.3\sqrt{0.5}} = 0.4186$$
$$d_2 = d_1 - 0.3\sqrt{0.5} = 0.2064$$

$$N(d_1) = 0.6622; \quad N(d_2) = 0.5818$$
$$N(-d_1) = 0.3378; \quad N(-d_2) = 0.4182$$

The value of one put option is

$$1140e^{-r(T-t)}N(-d_2) - 1200e^{-q(T-t)}N(-d_1)$$
$$=285e^{-0.06\times0.5} \times 0.4182 - 300e^{-0.03\times0.5} \times 0.3378$$
$$=63.40$$

The total cost of the insurance is therefore

$$300,000 \times 63.40 = \$19,020,000$$

(b) From put–call parity

$$S_0e^{-qT} + p = c + Xe^{-rT}$$

or:

$$p = c - S_0e^{-qT} + Xe^{-rT}$$

This shows that a put option can be created by selling (or shorting) e^{-qT} of the index, buying a call option and investing the remainder at the risk-free rate of interest. Applying this to the situation under consideration, the fund manager should:
1) Sell $360e^{-0.03\times0.5} = \$354.64$ million of stock
2) Buy 300,000 call options on the S&P 500 with exercise price 1140 and maturity in six months.
3) Invest the remaining cash at the risk-free interest rate of 6% per annum.
This strategy gives the same result as buying put options directly.
(c) The delta of one put option is

$$e^{-qT}[N(d_1) - 1]$$
$$=e^{-0.03\times0.5}(0.6622 - 1)$$
$$- 0.3327$$

This indicates that 33.27% of the portfolio (i.e., \$119.77 million) should be initially sold and invested in risk-free securities.
(d) The delta of a nine-month index futures contract is

$$e^{(r-q)T} = e^{0.03\times0.75} = 1.023$$

The spot short position required is

$$\frac{119,770,000}{300} = 99,808$$

times the index. Hence a short position in

$$\frac{99,808}{1.023 \times 250} = 390$$

futures contracts is required.

13.17. When the value of the portfolio goes down 5% in six months, the total return from the portfolio, including dividends, in the six months is

$$-5 + 2 = -3\%$$

i.e., -6% per annum. This is 12% per annum less than the risk-free interest rate. Since the portfolio has a beta of 1.5 we would expect the market to provide a return of 8% per annum less than the risk-free interest rate, i.e., we would expect the market to provide a return of -2% per annum. Since dividends on the market index are 3% per annum, we would expect the market index to have dropped at the rate of 5% per annum or 2.5% per six months; i.e., we would expect the market to have dropped to 1170. A total of $450,000 = (1.5 \times 300,000)$ put options on the S&P 500 with exercise price 1170 and exercise date in six months are therefore required.

(a) $S_0 = 1200$, $X = 1170$, $r = 0.06$, $\sigma = 0.3$, $T = 0.5$ and $q = 0.03$. Hence

$$d_1 = \frac{\ln(1200/1170) + (0.06 - 0.03 + 0.09/2) \times 0.5}{0.3\sqrt{0.5}} = 0.2961$$

$$d_2 = d_1 - 0.3\sqrt{0.5} = 0.0840$$

$$N(d_1) = 0.6164; \quad N(d_2) = 0.5335$$

$$N(-d_1) = 0.3836; \quad N(-d_2) = 0.4665$$

The value of one put option is

$$Xe^{-rT}N(-d_2) - S_0 e^{-qT}N(-d_1)$$
$$= 1170e^{-0.06 \times 0.5} \times 0.4665 - 1200e^{-0.03 \times 0.5} \times 0.3836$$
$$= 76.28$$

The total cost of the insurance is therefore

$$450,000 \times 76.28 = \$34,326,000$$

Note that this is significantly greater than the cost of the insurance in problem 13.16.

(b) As in problem 13.16 the fund manager can 1) sell \$354.64 million of stock, 2) buy 450,000 call options on the S&P 500 with exercise price 1170 and exercise date in six months and 3) invest the remaining cash at the risk-free interest rate.

(c) The portfolio is 50% more volatile than the S&P 500. When the insurance is considered as an option on the portfolio the parameters are as follows: $S_0 = 360$, $X = 342$, $r = 0.06$, $\sigma = 0.45$, $T = 0.5$ and $q = 0.04$

$$d_1 = \frac{\ln(360/342) + (0.06 - 0.04 + 0.45^2/2) \times 0.5}{0.45\sqrt{0.5}} = 0.3517$$

$$N(d_1) = 0.6374$$

The delta of the option is

$$e^{-qT}[N(d_1) - 1]$$
$$= e^{-0.03 \times 0.5}(0.6474 - 1)$$
$$= -0.355$$

This indicates that 35.5% of the portfolio (i.e., \$127.8 million) should be sold and invested in riskless securities.

(d) We now return to the situation considered in (a) where put options on the index are required. The delta of each put option is

$$e^{-qT}(N(d_1) - 1)$$
$$= e^{-0.03 \times 0.5}(0.6164 - 1)$$
$$= -0.3779$$

The delta of the total position required in put options is $-450,000 \times 0.3779 = -170,000$. The delta of a nine month index futures is (see problem 13.17) 1.023. Hence a short position in

$$\frac{170,000}{1.023 \times 250} = 665$$

index futures contracts.

13.18. (a) For a call option on a non-dividend-paying stock

$$\Delta = N(d_1)$$
$$\Gamma = \frac{N'(d_1)}{S_0 \sigma \sqrt{T}}$$
$$\Theta = -\frac{S_0 N'(d_1) \sigma}{2\sqrt{T}} - rX e^{-rT} N(d_2)$$

Hence the left-hand side of equation (13.7) is:

$$= -\frac{S_0 N'(d_1) \sigma}{2\sqrt{T}} - rX e^{-rT} N(d_2) + rS_0 N(d_1) + \frac{1}{2}\sigma S_0 \frac{N'(d_1)}{\sqrt{T}}$$
$$= r[S_0 N(d_1) - X e^{-rT)} N(d_2)]$$
$$= r\Pi$$

(b) For a put option on a non-dividend-paying stock

$$\Delta = N(d_1) - 1 = -N(-d_1)$$
$$\Gamma = \frac{N'(d_1)}{S_0 \sigma \sqrt{T}}$$
$$\Theta = -\frac{S_0 N'(d_1) \sigma}{2\sqrt{T}} + rX e^{-rT} N(-d_2)$$

Hence the left-hand side of equation (13.7) is:

$$-\frac{S_0 N'(d_1)\sigma}{2\sqrt{T}} + rXe^{-rT}N(-d_2) - rS_0N(-d_1) + \frac{1}{2}\sigma S_0 \frac{N'(d_1)}{\sqrt{T}}$$
$$=r[Xe^{-rT}N(-d_2) - S_0N(-d_1)]$$
$$=r\Pi$$

(c) For a portfolio of options, Π, Δ, Θ and Γ are the sums of their values for the individual options in the portfolio. It follows that equation (13.7) is true for any portfolio of European put and call options.

13.19. A currency is analogous to a stock paying a continuous dividend yield at rate r_f. The differential equation for a portfolio of derivatives dependent on a currency is

$$\frac{\partial \Pi}{\partial t} + (r - r_f)S\frac{\partial \Pi}{\partial S} + \frac{1}{2}\sigma^2 S^2 \frac{\partial^2 \Pi}{\partial S^2} = r\Pi$$

Hence

$$\Theta + (r - r_f)S\Delta + \frac{1}{2}\sigma^2 S^2\Gamma = r\Pi$$

Similarly, for a portfolio of derivatives dependent on a futures price

$$\Theta + \frac{1}{2}\sigma^2 S^2\Gamma = r\Pi$$

13.20. We can regard the position of all portfolio insurers taken together as a single put option. The three known parameters of the option, before the 23% decline, are $S_0 = 70$, $X = 66.5$, $T = 1$. Other parameters can be estimated as $r = 0.06$, $\sigma = 0.25$ and $q = 0.03$. Then:

$$d_1 = \frac{\ln(70/66.5) + (0.06 - 0.03 + 0.25^2/2)}{0.25} = 0.4502$$

$$N(d_1) = 0.6737$$

The delta of the option is
$$e^{-qT}[N(d_1) - 1]$$
$$=e^{-0.03\times0.5}(0.6737 - 1)$$
$$=-0.3167$$

This shows that 31.67% or $22.17 billion of assets should have been sold before the decline.
After the decline, $S_0 = 53.9$, $X = 66.5$, $T = 1$, $r = 0.06$, $\sigma = 0.25$ and $q = 0.03$.

$$d_1 = \frac{\ln(53.9/66.5) + (0.06 - 0.03 + 0.25^2/2)}{0.25} = -0.5953$$

$$N(d_1) = 0.2758$$

The delta of the option has dropped to

$$e^{-0.03 \times 0.5}(0.2758 - 1)$$
$$= -0.7028$$

This shows that cumulatively 70.28% or \$49.20 billion of assets (measured at their pre-crash prices) should be sold. In other words about \$27 billion of additional assets should be sold as a result of the decline.

13.21. With our usual notation the value of a forward contract on the asset is $S_0 e^{-qT} - K e^{-rT}$. When there is a small change, ΔS, in S_0 the value of the forward contract changes by $e^{-qT} \Delta S$. The delta of the forward contract is therefore e^{-qT}. The futures price is $S_0 e^{(r-q)T}$. When there is a small change, ΔS, in S_0 the futures price changes by $\Delta S e^{(r-q)T}$. Given the daily settlement procedures in futures contracts, this is also the immediate change in the wealth of the holder of the futures contract. The delta of the futures contract is therefore $e^{(r-q)T}$. We conclude that the deltas of a futures and forward contract are not the same. The delta of the futures is greater than the delta of the corresponding forward by a factor of e^{rT}.

13.22. The delta indicates that when the value of the euro exchange rate increases by \$0.01, the value of the bank's position increases by $0.01 \times 30,000 = \$300$. The gamma indicates that when the euro exchange rate increases by \$0.01 the delta of the portfolio decreases by $0.01 \times 80,000 = 800$. For delta neutrality 30,000 euros should be shorted. When the exchange rate moves up to 0.93, we expect the delta of the portfolio to decrease by $(0.93 - 0.90) \times 80,000 = 2,400$ so that it becomes 27,600. To maintain delta neutrality, it is therefore necessary for the bank to unwind its short position 2,400 euros so that a net 27,600 have been shorted. As shown in the text (see Figure 13.8), when a portfolio is delta neutral and has a negative gamma, a loss is experienced when there is a large movement in the underlying asset price price. We can conclude that the bank is likely to have lost money.

CHAPTER 14
Value at Risk

14.1. The standard deviation of the daily change in the investment in each asset is $1,000. The variance of the portfolio's daily change is

$$1,000^2 + 1,000^2 + 2 \times 0.3 \times 1,000 \times 1,000 = 2,600,000$$

The standard deviation of the portfolio's daily change is the square root of this or $1,612.45. The standard deviation of the 5-day change is

$$1,612.45 \times \sqrt{5} = \$3,605.55$$

From the tables of $N(x)$ we see that $N(-1.645) = 0.05$. This means that 5% of a normal distribution lies more than 1.645 standard deviations below the mean. The 5-day 95 percent value at risk is therefore $1.645 \times 3,605.55 = \$5,931$.

14.2. The duration model gives

$$\frac{\Delta B}{B} = -D\Delta y$$

where ΔB and Δy are the change in the value of the bond portfolio and its yield in one day, and D is the modified duration of the portfolio. Since $D = 3.7$ and the standard deviation of Δy is 0.09%, it follows that the standard deviation of the return on the bond portfolio in one day is $0.09 \times 3.7 = 0.3332\%$. The value of the portfolio is $4 million. The standard deviation of the change in its value in one day is therefore $4,000,000 \times 0.003332 = \$13,320$. Since $N(-1.282) = 0.9$, the 20-day 90 percent value at risk is

$$13,320 \times \sqrt{20} \times 1.282 = \$76,367$$

14.3. The approximate relationship beween the daily change in the portfolio value, ΔP, and the daily change in the exchange rate, ΔS, is

$$\Delta P = 56\Delta S$$

The proportional daily change in the exchange rate, Δx, equals $\Delta S/1.5$. It follows that

$$\Delta P = 56 \times 1.5\Delta x$$

or

$$\Delta P = 84\Delta x$$

The standard deviation of Δx equals the daily volatility of the exchange rate, or 0.7 percent. The standard deviation of ΔP is therefore $84 \times 0.007 = 0.588$. It follows that the 10-day 99 percent VaR for the portfolio is

$$0.588 \times 2.33 \times \sqrt{10} = 4.33$$

14.4. The relationship is

$$\Delta P = 56 \times 1.5\Delta x + \frac{1}{2} \times 1.5^2 \times 16.2 \times \Delta x^2$$

or

$$\Delta P = 84\Delta x + 18.225\Delta x^2$$

The first two moments of ΔP are

$$\frac{1}{2} \times 1.5^2 \times 16.2 \times 0.007^2 = 0.000893$$

and

$$1.5^2 \times 56^2 \times 0.007^2 + \frac{3}{4} \times 1.5^4 \times 16.2^2 \times 0.007^4 = 0.346$$

The mean and standard deviation of ΔP are therefore 0.000893 and $\sqrt{0.346 - 0.000893^2}$ = 0.588, respectively. The 10-day 99% VaR is therefore

$$\sqrt{10}(2.33 \times 0.588 - 0.000893) = 4.33$$

14.5. The factors calculated from a principal components analysis are uncorrelated. The daily variance of the portfolio is

$$6^2 \times 20^2 + 4^2 \times 8^2 = 15,424$$

and the daily standard deviation is $\sqrt{15,424} = \$124.19$. Since $N(-1.282) = 0.9$, the 5-day 90% value at risk is

$$124.19 \times \sqrt{5} \times 1.282 = \$356.01$$

14.6. The linear model assumes that the percentage daily change in each market variable has a normal probability distribution. The historical data model assumes that the probability distribution observed for the percentage daily changes in the market variables in the past is the probability distribution that will apply over the next day.

14.7. When a final exchange of principal is added in, the floating side is equivalent a zero coupon bond with a maturity date equal to the date of the next payment. The fixed side is a coupon-bearing bond, which is equivalent to a portfolio of zero-coupon bonds. The swap can therefore be mapped into a portfolio of zero-coupon bonds with maturity dates corresponding to the payment dates. Each of the zero-coupon bonds can then be mapped into positions in the adjacent standard-maturity zero-coupon bonds.

14.8. The change in the value of an option is not linearly related to the change in the value of the underlying variables. When the change in the values of underlying variables is normal, the change in the value of the option is non-normal. The linear model assumes that it is normal and is, therefore, only an approximation.

14.9. The 0.3-year cash flow is mapped into a 3-month zero-coupon bond and a 6-month zero-coupon bond. The 0.25 and 0.50 year rates are 5.50 and 6.00 respectively. Linear interpolation gives the 0.30-year rate as 5.60%. The present value of $50,000 received at time 0.3 years is

$$\frac{50,000}{1.056^{0.30}} = 49,189.32$$

The volatility of 0.25-year and 0.50-year zero-coupon bonds are 0.06% and 0.10% per day respectively. The interpolated volatility of a 0.30-year zero-coupon bond is therefore 0.068% per day.

Assume that α of the value of the 0.30-year cash flow gets allocated to a 3-month zero-coupon bond and $1 - \alpha$ to a six-month zero coupon bond. To match variances we must have

$$0.00068^2 = 0.0006^2\alpha^2 + 0.001^2(1-\alpha)^2 + 2 \times 0.9 \times 0.0006 \times 0.001\alpha(1-\alpha)$$

or

$$0.28\alpha^2 - 0.92\alpha + 0.5376 = 0$$

Using the formula for the solution to a quadratic equation

$$\alpha = \frac{-0.92 + \sqrt{0.92^2 - 4 \times 0.28 \times 0.5376}}{2 \times 0.28} = 0.760259$$

this means that a value of $0.760259 \times 49,189.32 = \$37,397$ is allocated to the three-month bond and a value of $0.239741 \times 49,189.32 = \$11,793$ is allocated to the six-month bond. The 0.3-year cash flow is therefore equivalent to a position of $37,397 in a 3-month zero-coupon bond and a position of $11,793 in a 6-month zero-coupon bond. This is consistent with the results in Table 14.2 of the text.

14.10. The 6.5-year cash flow is mapped into a 5-year zero-coupon bond and a 7-year zero-coupon bond. The 5-year and 7-year rates are 6% and 7% respectively. Linear interpolation gives the 6.5-year rate as 6.75%. The present value of $1,000 received at time 6.5 years is

$$\frac{1,000}{1.0675^{6.5}} = 654.05$$

The volatility of 5-year and 7-year zero-coupon bonds are 0.50% and 0.58% per day respectively. The interpolated volatility of a 6.5-year zero-coupon bond is therefore 0.056% per day.

Assume that α of the value of the 6.5-year cash flow gets allocated to a 5-year zero-coupon bond and $1 - \alpha$ to a 7-year zero coupon bond. To match variances we must have

$$.56^2 = .50^2\alpha^2 + .58^2(1-\alpha)^2 + 2 \times 0.6 \times .50 \times .58\alpha(1-\alpha)$$

or

$$.2384\alpha^2 - .3248\alpha + .0228 = 0$$

Using the formula for the solution to a quadratic equation

$$\alpha = \frac{.3248 - \sqrt{.3248^2 - 4 \times .2384 \times .0228}}{2 \times .2384} = 0.074243$$

this means that a value of $0.074243 \times 654.05 = \$48.56$ is allocated to the 5-year bond and a value of $0.925757 \times 654.05 = \$605.49$ is allocated to the 7-year bond. The 6.5-year cash flow is therefore equivalent to a position of \$48.56 in a 3-month zero-coupon bond and a position of \$605.49 in a 7-year zero-coupon bond.

The equivalent 5-year and 7-year cash flows are $48.56 \times 1.06^5 = 64.98$ and $605.49 \times 1.07^7 = 972.28$.

14.11. The contract is a long position in a sterling bond combined with a short position in a dollar bond. The value of the sterling bond is $1.53e^{-0.05 \times 0.5}$ or \$1.492 million. The value of the dollar bond is $1.5e^{-0.05 \times 0.5}$ or \$1.463 million. The variance of the change in the value of the contract in one day is

$$1.492^2 \times 0.0006^2 + 1.463^2 \times 0.0005^2 - 2 \times 0.8 \times 1.492 \times 0.0006 \times 1.463 \times 0.0005$$

$$= 0.000000288$$

The standard deviation is therefore \$0.000537 million. The 10-day 99% VaR is $0.000537 \times \sqrt{10} \times 2.33 = \$0.00396$ million.

14.12. If we assume only one factor, the model is

$$\Delta P = -0.08 f_1$$

The standard deviation of f_1 is 17.49. The standard deviation of ΔP is therefore $0.08 \times 17.49 = 1.40$ and the 1-day 99 percent value at risk is $1.40 \times 2.33 = 3.26$. If we assume three factors, our exposure to the third factor is

$$10 \times (-0.37) + 4 \times (-0.38) - 8 \times (-0.30) - 7 \times (-0.12) + 2 \times (-0.04) = -2.06$$

The model is therefore

$$\Delta P = -0.08 f_1 - 4.40 f_2 - 2.06 f_3$$

The variance of ΔP is

$$0.08^2 \times 17.49^2 + 4.40^2 \times 6.05^2 + 2.06^2 \times 3.1062 = 751.36$$

The standard deviation of ΔP is $\sqrt{751.36} = 27.41$ and the 1-day 99% value at risk is $27.41 \times 2.33 = \$63.87$.

The example illustrates that the relative importance of different factors depends on the portfolio being considered. Normally the second factor is less important than the first, but in this case it is much more important.

14.13. The delta of the options is the rate if change of the value of the options with respect to the price of the asset. When the asset price increases by a small amount the value of the options decrease by 30 times this amount. The gamma of the options is the rate of change of their delta with respect to the price of the asset. When the asset price increases by a small amount, the delta of the portfolio decreases by five times this amount.

Suppose that ΔS is the change in the asset price in one day and Δx is the proportional change in the asset price. The delta–gamma model is

$$\Delta P = -30\Delta S - .5 \times 5 \times (\Delta S)^2$$

or

$$\Delta P = -30 \times 20\Delta x - 0.5 \times 5 \times 20^2 \times (\Delta x)^2$$

which simplifies to

$$\Delta P = -600\Delta x - 1,000(\Delta x)^2$$

From the equations in section 14.6 of the text the first three moments of the portfolio value are

$$\frac{1}{2} \times 20^2 \times (-5) \times 0.01^2 = -0.1$$

$$20^2 \times 30^2 \times 0.01^2 + \frac{3}{4} \times 20^4 \times 5^2 \times 0.01^4 = 36.03$$

and

$$\frac{9}{2} \times 20^4 \times 30^2 \times (-5) \times 0.01^4 + \frac{15}{8} \times 20^6 \times (-5)^3 \times 0.01^6 = -32.415$$

The mean change in the portfolio value in one day is -0.1 and the standard deviation of the change in one day is $\sqrt{36.03 - 0.1^2} = 6.002$. The skewness is

$$\frac{-32.415 - 3 \times 36.03 \times (-0.1) + 2 \times (-0.1)^3}{6.002^3} = -21.608 = -0.10$$

Using only the first two moments the 1-day 99% value at risk is therefore $0.1 + 2.33 \times 6.002 = \$14.08$

When three moments Appendix 14A shows that the 1 percentile of the distribution is

$$-0.1 - 6.002w_q$$

where

$$w_q = -2.33 + \frac{1}{6} \times (2.33^2 - 1) \times (-0.1) = 2.404$$

The one percentile point is therefore $-0.1 - 6.002 \times 2.404 = -14.529$ showing that the 1-day 99% VaR is 14.529.

14.13. Define σ as the volatility per year, $\Delta\sigma$ as the change in σ in one day, and Δw and the proportional change in σ in one day. We measure in σ as a multiple of 1% so that the current value of σ is $1 \times \sqrt{252} = 15.87$. The delta-gamma-vega model is

$$\Delta P = -30\Delta S - .5 \times 5 \times (\Delta S)^2 - 2\Delta\sigma$$

or

$$\Delta P = -30 \times 20\Delta x - 0.5 \times 5 \times 20^2(\Delta x)^2 - 2 \times 15.87\Delta w$$

which simplifies to

$$\Delta P = -600\Delta x - 1,000(\Delta x)^2 - 31.74\Delta w$$

The change in the portfolio value now depends on two market variables. Once the daily volatiliity of σ and the correlation between σ and S have been estimated we can use the results in Appendix 14A to estimate moments of ΔP. An alternative approach is would be to use Monte Carlo simulation in conjunction with the model.

CHAPTER 15
Estimating Volatilities and Correlations

15.1. Define u_i as $(S_i - S_{i-1})/S_{i-1}$, where S_i is value of a market variable on day i. In the EWMA model, the variance rate of the market variable (i.e., the square of its volatility) calculated for day n is a weighted average of the u_{n-i}^2's ($i = 1, 2, 3, \ldots$). For some constant λ ($0 < \lambda < 1$) the weight given to u_{n-i-1}^2 is λ times the the weight given to u_{n-i}^2. The volatility estimated for day n, σ_n, is related to the volatility estimated for day $n-1$, σ_{n-1}, by

$$\sigma_n^2 = \lambda \sigma_{n-1}^2 + (1 - \lambda) u_{n-1}^2$$

This formula shows that the EWMA model has one very attractive property. To calculate the volatility estimate for day n, it is sufficient to know the volatility estimate for day $n-1$ and u_n.

15.2. The EWMA model produces a forecast of the daily variance rate for day n which is a weighted average of (i) the forecast for day $n-1$, and (ii) the square of the proportional change on day $n-1$. The GARCH (1,1) model produces a forecast of the daily variance for day n which is a weighted average of (i) the forecast for day $n-1$, (ii) the square of the proportional change on day $n-1$. and (iii) a long run average variance rate. GARCH (1,1) adapts the EWMA model by giving some weight to a long run average variance rate. Whereas the EWMA has no mean reversion, GARCH (1,1) is consistent with a mean-reverting variance rate model.

15.3. In this case $\sigma_{n-1} = 0.015$ and $u_n = 0.5/30 = 0.01667$, so that equation (15.7) gives

$$\sigma_n^2 = 0.94 \times 0.015^2 + 0.06 \times 0.01667^2 = 0.0002281$$

The volatility estimate on day n is therefore $\sqrt{0.0002281} = 0.015103$ or 1.5103%.

15.4. Reducing λ from 0.95 to 0.85 means that more weight is put on recent observations of u_i^2 and less weight is given to older observations. Volatilities calculated with $\lambda = 0.85$ will react more quickly to new information and will "bounce around" much more than volatilities calculated with $\lambda = 0.95$.

15.5. The volatilty per day is $30/\sqrt{252} = 1.89\%$. There is a 99% chance that a normally distributed variable will lie within 2.57 standard deviations. We are therefore 99% confident that the daily change will be less than $2.57 \times 1.89 = 4.86\%$.

15.6. The weight given to the long-run average variance rate is $1 - \alpha - \beta$ and the long-run average variance rate is $\omega/(1 - \alpha - \beta)$. Increasing ω increases the long-run average variance rate; Increasing α increases the weight given to the most recent data item, reduces the weight given to the long-run average variance rate, and increases the level of the long-run average variance rate. Increasing β increases the weight given to the previous variance estimate, reduces the weight given to the long-run average variance rate, and increases the level of the long-run average variance rate.

15.7. The proportional daily change is $-0.005/1.5000 = -0.003333$. The current daily variance estimate is $0.006^2 = 0.000036$. The new daily variance estimate is

$$0.9 \times 0.000036 + 0.1 \times 0.003333^2 = 0.000033511$$

The new volatility is the square root of this. It is 0.00579 or 0.579%.

15.8. With the usual notation $u_{n-1} = 20/1040 = 0.01923$ so that

$$\sigma_n^2 = 0.000002 + 0.06 \times 0.01923^2 + 0.92 \times 0.01^2 = 0.0001342$$

so that $\sigma_n = 0.01158$. The new volatility estimate is therefore 1.158% per day.

15.9. (a) The volatilities and correlation imply that the current estimate of the covariance is $0.25 \times 0.016 \times 0.025 = 0.0001$.
(b) If the prices of the assets at close of trading are \$20.5 and \$40.5, the proportional changes are $0.5/20 = 0.025$ and $0.5/40 = 0.0125$. The new covariance estimate is

$$0.95 \times 0.0001 + 0.05 \times 0.025 \times 0.0125 = 0.0001106$$

The new variance estimate for asset A is

$$0.95 \times 0.016^2 + 0.05 \times 0.025^2 = 0.00027445$$

so that the new volatility is 0.0166. The new variance estimate for asset B is

$$0.95 \times 0.025^2 + 0.05 \times 0.0125^2 = 0.000601562$$

so that the new volatility is 0.0245. The new correlation estimate is

$$\frac{0.0001106}{0.0166 \times 0.0245} = 0.272$$

15.10. The long-run average variance rate is $\omega/(1 - \alpha - \beta)$ or $0.000004/0.03 = 0.0001333$. The long-run average volatility is $\sqrt{0.0001333}$ or 1.155%. The equation describing the way the variance rate reverts to its long-run average is equation (15.13)

$$E[\sigma_{n+k}^2] = V + (\alpha + \beta)^k (\sigma_n^2 - V)$$

In this case
$$E[\sigma_{n+k}^2] = 0.0001333 + 0.97^k(\sigma_n^2 - 0.0001333)$$

If the current volatility is 20% per year, $\sigma_n = 0.2/\sqrt{252} = 0.0126$. The expected variance rate in 20 days is

$$0.0001333 + 0.97^{20}(0.0126^2 - 0.0001333) = 0.0001471$$

The expected volatility in 20 days is therefore $\sqrt{0.0001471} = 0.0121$ or 1.21% per day.

15.11. Using the notation in the text $\sigma_{u,n-1} = 0.01$ and $\sigma_{v,n-1} = 0.012$ and the most recent estimate of the covariance between the asset returns is $\text{cov}_{n-1} = 0.01 \times 0.012 \times 0.50 = 0.00006$. The variable $u_{n-1} = 1/30 = 0.03333$ and the variable $v_{n-1} = 1/50 = 0.02$. The new estimate of the covariance, cov_n, is

$$0.000001 + 0.04 \times 0.03333 \times 0.02 + 0.94 \times 0.00006 = 0.0000841$$

The new estimate of the variance of the first asset, $\sigma_{u,n}^2$ is

$$0.000003 + 0.04 \times 0.03333^2 + 0.94 \times 0.01^2 = 0.0001414$$

so that $\sigma_{u,n} = \sqrt{0.0001414} = 0.01189$ or 1.189%. The new estimate of the variance of the second asset, $\sigma_{v,n}^2$ is

$$0.000003 + 0.04 \times 0.02^2 + 0.94 \times 0.012^2 = 0.0001544$$

so that $\sigma_{v,n} = \sqrt{0.0001544} = 0.01242$ or 1.242%. The new estimate of the correlation between the assets is therefore $0.0000841/(0.01189 \times 0.01242) = 0.569$.

15.12. The FT-SE expressed in dollars is XY where X is the FT-SE expressed in sterling and Y is the exchange rate (value of one pound in dollars). Define x_i as the proportional change in X on day i and y_i as the proportional change in Y on day i. The proportional change in XY is approximately $x_i + y_i$. The standard deviation of x_i is 0.018 and the standard deviation of y_i is 0.009. The correlation between the two is 0.4. The variance of $x_i + y_i$ is therefore

$$0.018^2 + 0.009^2 + 2 \times 0.018 \times 0.009 \times 0.4 = 0.0005346$$

so that the volatility of $x_i + y_i$ is 0.0231 or 2.31%. This is the volatility of the FT-SE expressed in dollars. Note that it is greater than the volatility of the FT-SE expressed in sterling. This is the impact of the positive correlation. When the FT-SE increases the value of sterling measured in dollars also tends to increase. This creates an even bigger increase in the value of FT-SE measured in dollars. Similarly for a decrease in the FT-SE.

15.13. Continuing with the notation in Problem 15.12, define z_i as the proportional change in the value of the S&P 500 on day i. The covariance between x_i and z_i is $0.7 \times 0.018 \times$

$0.016 = 0.0002016$. The covariance between y_i and z_i is $0.3 \times 0.009 \times 0.016 = 0.0000432$. The covariance between $x_i + y_i$ and z_i equals the covariance between x_i and z_i plus the covariance between y_i and z_i. It is

$$0.0002016 + 0.0000432 = 0.0002448$$

The correlation between $x_i + y_i$ and z_i is

$$\frac{0.0002448}{0.016 \times 0.0231} = 0.662$$

CHAPTER 16
Numerical Procedures

16.1. Delta, gamma, and theta can be determined from a single binomial tree. Vega is determined by making a small change to the volatility and recomputing the option price using a new tree. Rho is calculated by making a small change to the interest rate and recomputing the option price using a new tree.

16.2. In this case, $S = 60$, $X = 60$, $r = 0.1$, $\sigma = 0.45$, $T = 0.25$, and $\Delta t = 0.0833$. Also

$$u = e^{\sigma\sqrt{\Delta t}} = e^{0.45\sqrt{0.0833}} = 1.1387$$

$$d = \frac{1}{u} = 0.8782$$

$$a = e^{r\Delta t} = e^{0.1 \times 0.0833} = 1.0084$$

$$p = \frac{a - u}{u - d} = 0.4998$$

$$1 - p = 0.5002$$

The output from DerivaGem for this example is shown in the Figure 16.1. The calculated price of the option is $5.16.

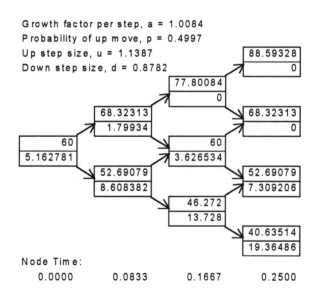

Growth factor per step, a = 1.0084
Probability of up move, p = 0.4997
Up step size, u = 1.1387
Down step size, d = 0.8782

Node Time:
0.0000   0.0833   0.1667   0.2500

Figure 16.1   Tree for Problem 16.2

16.3. The control variate technique is implemented by
   (a) valuing an American option using a binomial tree in the usual way ($= f_A$).
   (b) valuing the European option with the same parameters as the American option using the same tree ($= f_E$).
   (c) valuing the European option using Black–Scholes ($= f_{BS}$).
   The price of the American option is estimated as $f_A + f_{BS} - f_E$.

16.4. In this case $F = 198$, $X = 200$, $r = 0.08$, $\sigma = 0.3$, $T = 0.75$, and $\Delta t = 0.25$. Also

$$u = e^{0.3\sqrt{0.25}} = 1.1618$$

$$d = \frac{1}{u} = 0.8607$$

$$a = 1$$

$$p = \frac{a - d}{u - d} = 0.4626$$

$$1 - p = 0.5373$$

The output from DerivaGem for this example is shown in the Figure 16.2. The calculated price of the option is 20.34 cents.

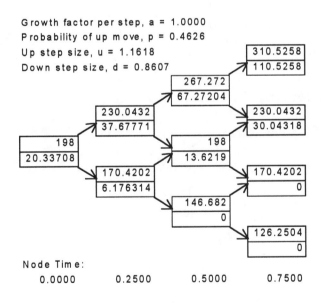

Growth factor per step, a = 1.0000
Probability of up move, p = 0.4626
Up step size, u = 1.1618
Down step size, d = 0.8607

310.5258
110.5258

267.272
67.27204

230.0432
37.67771

230.0432
30.04318

198
20.33708

198
13.6219

170.4202
6.176314

170.4202
0

146.682
0

126.2504
0

Node Time:
0.0000   0.2500   0.5000   0.7500

Figure 16.2   Tree for Problem 16.4

16.5. A binomial tree cannot be used in the way described in this chapter. This is an example of what is known as a history-dependent option. The payoff depends on the path followed by the stock price as well as its final value. The option cannot be valued by starting at the end of the tree and working backward since the payoff at the final branches is not known unambiguously. Chapter 18 describes an extension of the binomial tree approach that can be used to handle options where the payoff depends on the average value of the stock price.

16.6. Suppose a dividend equal to D is paid during a certain time interval. If S is the stock price at the beginning of the time interval, it will be either $Su - D$ or $Sd - D$ at the end of the time interval. At the end of the next time interval, it will be one of $(Su - D)u$, $(Su - D)d$, $(Sd - D)u$ and $(Sd - D)d$. Since $(Su - D)d$ does not equal $(Sd - D)u$ the tree does not recombine. If S is equal to the stock price less the present value of future dividends, this problem is avoided.

16.7. With the usual notation

$$p = \frac{a - d}{u - d}$$

$$1 - p = \frac{u - a}{u - d}$$

If $a < d$ or $a > u$, one of the two probabilities is negative. This happens when

$$e^{(r-q)\Delta t} < e^{-\sigma\sqrt{\Delta t}}$$

or

$$e^{(r-q)\Delta t} > e^{\sigma\sqrt{\Delta t}}$$

This in turn happens when $(q - r)\sqrt{\Delta t} > \sigma$ or $(r - q)\sqrt{\Delta t} > \sigma$ Hence negative probabilities occur when

$$\sigma < |(r - q)\sqrt{\Delta t}|$$

This is the condition in footnote 8.

16.8. When the dividend yield is constant

$$u = e^{\sigma\sqrt{\Delta t}}$$

$$d = \frac{1}{u}$$

$$p = \frac{a - d}{u - d}$$

$$a = e^{(r-q)\Delta t}$$

Making the dividend yield, q, a function of time makes a, and therefore p, a function of time. However, it does not affect u or d. It follows that if q is a function of time we can use the same tree by making the probabilities a function of time. The interest rate r can also be a function of time as described in Section 16.4.

16.9. In Monte Carlo simulation sample values for the derivative security in a risk-neutral world are obtained by simulating paths for the underlying variables. On each simulation run, values for the underlying variables are first determined at time Δt, then at time $2\Delta t$, then at time $3\Delta t$, etc. At time $i\Delta t$ $(i = 0, 1, 2 \ldots)$ it is not possible to determine whether early exercise is optimal since the range of paths which might occur after time $i\Delta t$ have not been investigated. In short, Monte Carlo simulation works by moving forward from time t to time T. Other numerical procedures which accommodate early exercise work by moving backwards from time T to time t.

16.10. In this case, $S = 50$, $X = 49$, $r = 0.05$, $\sigma = 0.30$, $T = 0.75$, and $\Delta t = 0.25$. Also

$$u = e^{\sigma\sqrt{\Delta t}} = e^{0.30\sqrt{0.25}} = 1.0126$$

$$d = \frac{1}{u} = 0.8607$$

$$a = e^{r\Delta t} = e^{0.1 \times 0.0833} = 1.0084$$

$$p = \frac{a - u}{u - d} = 0.5043$$

$$1 - p = 0.4957$$

The output from DerivaGem for this example is shown in the Figure 16.3. The calculated price of the option is \$4.29. Using 100 steps the price obtained is \$3.91

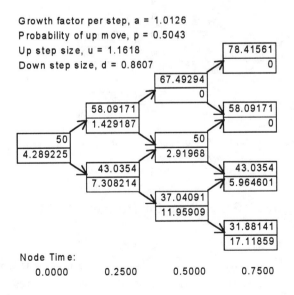

Growth factor per step, a = 1.0126
Probability of up move, p = 0.5043
Up step size, u = 1.1618
Down step size, d = 0.8607

			78.41561
			0
		67.49294	
		0	
	58.09171		58.09171
	1.429187		0
50		50	
4.289225		2.91968	
	43.0354		43.0354
	7.308214		5.964601
		37.04091	
		11.95909	
			31.88141
			17.11859

Node Time:
0.0000   0.2500   0.5000   0.7500

Figure 16.3   Tree for Problem 16.10

16.11. In this case $F = 400$, $X = 420$, $r = 0.06$, $\sigma = 0.35$, $T = 0.75$, and $\Delta t = 0.25$. Also

$$u = e^{0.35\sqrt{0.25}} = 1.1912$$

$$d = \frac{1}{u} = 0.8395$$

$$a = 1$$

$$p = \frac{a - d}{u - d} = 0.4564$$

$$1 - p = 0.5436$$

The output from DerivaGem for this example is shown in the Figure 16.4. The calculated price of the option is 42.07 cents. Using 100 time steps the price obtained is 38.64. The options delta is calculated from the tree is

$$(79.971 - 11.419)/(476.498 - 335.783) = 0.535$$

. When 100 steps are used the esimate of the option's delta is 0.483.

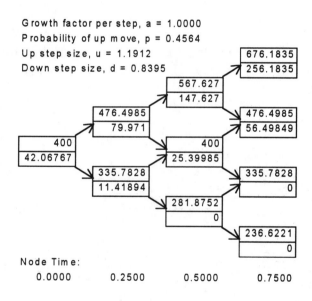

Growth factor per step, a = 1.0000
Probability of up move, p = 0.4564
Up step size, u = 1.1912
Down step size, d = 0.8395

Figure 16.4 Tree for Problem 16.11

16.12. In this case the present value of the dividend is $2e^{-0.03 \times 0.125} = 1.9925$. We first build a tree for $S = 20 - 1.9925 = 18.0075$, $X = 20$, $r = 0.03$, $\sigma = 0.25$, and $T = 0.25$ with $\Delta t = 0.08333$. This gives Figure 16.5. For nodes between times 0 and 1.5 months we then add the present value of the dividend to the stock price. The result is the tree in Figure 16.6. The price of the option calculated from the tree is 0.544. When 100 steps are used the price obtained is 0.551.

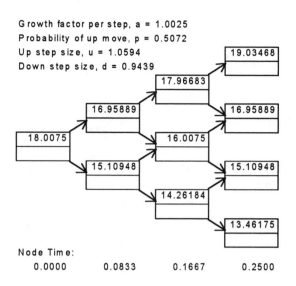

Growth factor per step, a = 1.0025
Probability of up move, p = 0.5072
Up step size, u = 1.0594
Down step size, d = 0.9439

Node Time:
0.0000   0.0833   0.1667   0.2500

Figure 16.5   First tree for Problem 16.12

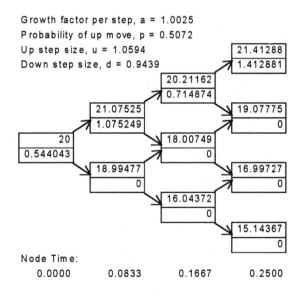

Growth factor per step, a = 1.0025
Probability of up move, p = 0.5072
Up step size, u = 1.0594
Down step size, d = 0.9439

Node Time:
0.0000   0.0833   0.1667   0.2500

Figure 16.6   Final Tree for Problem 16.12

16.13. In this case $S = 20$, $X = 18$, $r = 0.15$, $\sigma = 0.40$, $T = 1$, and $\Delta t = 0.25$. The

111

parameters for the tree are

$$u = e^{\sigma\sqrt{\Delta t}} = e^{0.4\sqrt{0.25}} = 1.2214$$

$$d = 1/u = 0.8187$$

$$a = e^{r\Delta t} = 1.0382$$

$$p = \frac{a-d}{u-d} = \frac{1.0382 - 0.8187}{1.2214 - 0.8187} = 0.545$$

The tree produced by DerivaGem for the American option is shown in Figure 16.7. The estimated value of the American option is $1.29.

As shown in Figure 16.8, the same tree can be used to value a European put option with the same parameters. The estimated value of the European option is $1.14. The option parameters are $S = 20$, $X = 18$, $r = 0.15$, $\sigma = 0.40$ and $T = 1$

$$d_1 = \frac{\ln(20/18) + 0.15 + 0.40^2/2}{0.40} = 0.8384$$

$$d_2 = d_1 - 0.40 = 0.4384$$

$$N(-d_1) = 0.2009; \quad N(-d_2) = 0.3306$$

The true European put price is therefore

$$18e^{-0.15} \times 0.3306 - 20 \times 0.2009 = 1.10$$

The control variate estimate of the American put price is therefore $1.29 + 1.10 - 1.14 = $1.25.

16.14. In this case $S = 484$, $X = 480$, $r = 0.10$, $\sigma = 0.25$ $q = 0.03$, $T = 0.1667$, and $\Delta t = 0.04167$

$$u = e^{\sigma\sqrt{\Delta t}} = e^{0.25\sqrt{0.04167}} = 1.0524$$

$$d = \frac{1}{u} = 0.9502$$

$$a = e^{(r-q)\Delta t} = 1.00292$$

$$p = \frac{a-d}{u-d} = \frac{1.0029 - 0.9502}{1.0524 - 0.9502} = 0.516$$

The tree produced by DerivaGem is shown in the Figure 16.9. The estimated price of the option is $14.93.

16.15. First the delta of the American option is estimated in the usual way from the tree. Denote this by Δ_A^*. Then the delta of a European option which has the same parameters as the American option is calculated in the same way using the same tree. Denote

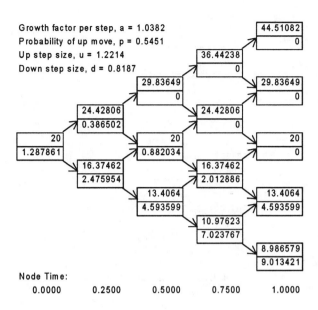

Growth factor per step, a = 1.0382
Probability of up move, p = 0.5451
Up step size, u = 1.2214
Down step size, d = 0.8187

Node Time:				
0.0000	0.2500	0.5000	0.7500	1.0000

Figure 16.7   Tree to evaluate American option for Problem 16.13

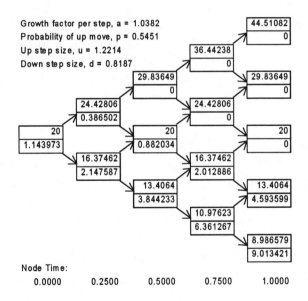

Growth factor per step, a = 1.0382
Probability of up move, p = 0.5451
Up step size, u = 1.2214
Down step size, d = 0.8187

Node Time:				
0.0000	0.2500	0.5000	0.7500	1.0000

Figure 16.8   Tree to evaluate European option in Problem 16.13

this by Δ_B^*. Finally the true European delta, Δ_B, is calculated using the formulas in Chapter 13. The control variate estimate of delta is then:

$$\Delta_A^* - \Delta_B^* + \Delta_B$$

113

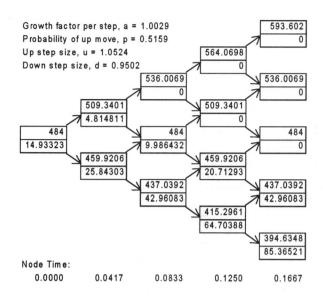

Growth factor per step, a = 1.0029
Probability of up move, p = 0.5159
Up step size, u = 1.0524
Down step size, d = 0.9502

| 593.602 |
| 0 |

| 564.0698 |
| 0 |

| 536.0069 |
| 0 |

| 536.0069 |
| 0 |

| 509.3401 |
| 4.814811 |

| 509.3401 |
| 0 |

| 484 |
| 14.93323 |

| 484 |
| 9.986432 |

| 484 |
| 0 |

| 459.9206 |
| 25.84303 |

| 459.9206 |
| 20.71293 |

| 437.0392 |
| 42.96083 |

| 437.0392 |
| 42.96083 |

| 415.2961 |
| 64.70388 |

| 394.6348 |
| 85.36521 |

Node Time:
0.0000   0.0417   0.0833   0.1250   0.1667

Figure 16.9   Tree to evaluate option in Problem 16.14

16.16. In this case a simulation requires two sets of samples from standardized normal distributions. The first is to generate the volatility movements. The second is to generate the stock price movements once the volatility movements are known. The control variate technique involves carrying out a second simulation on the assumption that the volatility is constant. The same random number stream is used to generate stock price movements as in the first simulation. An improved estimate of the option price is

$$f_A^* - f_B^* + f_B$$

where f_A^* is the option value from the first simulation (when the volatility is stochastic), f_B^* is the option value from the second simulation (when the volatility is constant) and f_B is the true Black-Scholes value when the volatility is constant.

To use the antithetic variable technique, two sets of samples from standardized normal distributions must be used for each of volatility and stock price. Denote the volatility samples by $\{V_1\}$ and $\{V_2\}$ and the stock price samples by $\{S_1\}$ and $\{S_2\}$. $\{V_1\}$ is antithetic to $\{V_2\}$ and $\{S_1\}$ is antithetic to $\{S_2\}$. Thus if

$$\{V_1\} = +0.83, +0.41, -0.21\ldots$$

then

$$\{V_2\} = -0.83, -0.41, +0.21\ldots$$

Similarly for $\{S_1\}$ and $\{S_2\}$.

An efficient way of proceeding is to carry out six simulations in parallel:

  Simulation 1: Use $\{S_1\}$ with volatility constant
  Simulation 2: Use $\{S_2\}$ with volatility constant

114

Simulation 3: Use $\{S_1\}$ and $\{V_1\}$
Simulation 4: Use $\{S_1\}$ and $\{V_2\}$
Simulation 5: Use $\{S_2\}$ and $\{V_1\}$
Simulation 6: Use $\{S_2\}$ and $\{V_2\}$

If f_i is the option price from simulation i, simulations 3 and 4 provide an estimate $0.5(f_3 + f_4)$ for the option price. When the control variate technique is used we combine this estimate with the result of simulation 1 to obtain $0.5(f_3 + f_4) - f_1 + f_B$ as an estimate of the price where f_B is, as above, the Black-Scholes option price. Similarly simulations 2, 5 and 6 provide an estimate $0.5(f_5 + f_6) - f_2 + f_B$. Overall the best estimate is:

$$0.5[0.5(f_3 + f_4) - f_1 + f_B + 0.5(f_5 + f_6) - f_2 + f_B]$$

16.17. For an American call option on a currency

$$\frac{\partial f}{\partial t} + (r - r_f)S\frac{\partial f}{\partial S} + \frac{1}{2}\sigma^2 S^2 \frac{\partial^2 f}{\partial S^2} = rf$$

With the notation in the text this becomes

$$\frac{f_{i+1,j} - f_{ij}}{\Delta t} + (r - r_f)j\Delta S \frac{f_{i,j+1} - f_{i,j-1}}{2\Delta S} + \frac{1}{2}\sigma^2 j^2 \Delta S^2 \frac{f_{i,j+1} - 2f_{i,j} + f_{i,j-1}}{\Delta S^2} = rf_{ij}$$

for $j = 1, 2 \ldots M - 1$ and $i = 0, 1 \ldots N - 1$. Rearranging terms we obtain

$$a_j f_{i,j-1} + b_j f_{ij} + c_j f_{i,j+1} = f_{i+1,j}$$

where

$$a_j = \frac{1}{2}(r - r_f)j\Delta t - \frac{1}{2}\sigma^2 j^2 \Delta t$$
$$b_j = 1 + \sigma^2 j^2 \Delta t + r\Delta t$$
$$c_j = -\frac{1}{2}(r - r_f)j\Delta t - \frac{1}{2}\sigma^2 j^2 \Delta t$$

Equations (16.26), (16.27) and (16.28) become

$$f_{Nj} = \max[j\Delta S - X, 0] \quad j = 0, 1 \ldots M$$
$$f_{i0} = 0 \quad i = 0, 1 \ldots N$$
$$f_{iM} = M\Delta S - X \quad i = 0, 1 \ldots N$$

16.18. We consider stock prices of \$0, \$4, \$8, \$12, \$16, \$20, \$24, \$28, \$32, \$36 and \$40. Using equation (16.32) with $r = 0.10$, $\Delta t = 0.0833$, $\Delta S = 4$, $\sigma = 0.30$, $S = 20$, $X = 21$, $T - t = 0.3333$ we obtain the table shown below. The option price is \$1.56.

Grid for Finite Difference Approach in Problem 16.18.

Stock Price ($)	Time To Maturity (Months)				
	4	3	2	1	0
40	0.00	0.00	0.00	0.00	0.00
36	0.00	0.00	0.00	0.00	0.00
32	0.01	0.00	0.00	0.00	0.00
28	0.07	0.04	0.02	0.00	0.00
24	0.38	0.30	0.21	0.11	0.00
20	1.56	1.44	1.31	1.17	1.00
16	5.00	5.00	5.00	5.00	5.00
12	9.00	9.00	9.00	9.00	9.00
8	13.00	13.00	13.00	13.00	13.00
4	17.00	17.00	17.00	17.00	17.00
0	21.00	21.00	21.00	21.00	21.00

16.19. In a risk-neutral world the process for r is

$$\frac{dr}{r} = \left[\frac{a(b-r)}{r} - \lambda c \right] dt + c\, dz$$

where λ is the market price of risk for r. The fact that the growth rate of r in a risk-neutral world is a function of r does create some problems. The parameters u and d in the binomial tree are not affected by the growth rate of the underlying variable (in this case $u = e^{c\sqrt{\Delta t}}, d = e^{-c\sqrt{\Delta t}}$). However the probability parameter, p, does depend on this growth rate. To be a valid probability p must be between 0.0 and 1.0. For high values of r, p is liable to be negative; for low values of r, p is liable to be greater than 1.0.

16.20. In this case $\Delta t = 0.25$ and $\sigma = 0.4$ so that

$$u = e^{0.4\sqrt{0.25}} = 1.2214$$

$$d = \frac{1}{u} = 0.8187$$

The futures prices provide estimates of the growth rate in copper in a risk-neutral world. During the first three months this growth rate (with continuous compounding) is

$$4 \ln \frac{0.59}{0.60} = -6.72\% \text{ per annum}$$

The parameter p for the first three months is therefore

$$\frac{e^{-0.0672 \times 0.25} - 0.8187}{1.2214 - 0.8187} = 0.4088$$

116

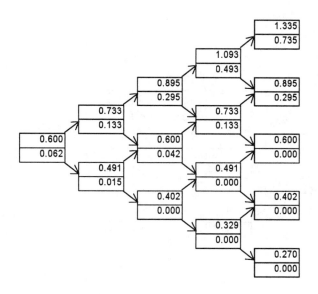

Figure 16.10   Tree to value option in Problem 16.20: At each node, upper number is price of copper and lower number is option price

The growth rate in copper is equal to −13.79%, −21.63% and −30.78% in the following three quarters. Therefore, the parameter p for the second three months is

$$\frac{e^{-0.1379 \times 0.25} - 0.8187}{1.2214 - 0.8187} = 0.3660$$

For the third quarter it is

$$\frac{e^{-0.2163 \times 0.25} - 0.8187}{1.2214 - 0.8187} = 0.3195$$

For the final quarter, it is

$$\frac{e^{-0.3078 \times 0.25} - 0.8187}{1.2214 - 0.8187} = 0.2663$$

The tree for the movements in copper prices in a risk-neutral world is shown in Figure 16.10. The value of the option is $0.062.

16.21. In this problem we use exactly the same tree for copper prices as in Problem 16.20. However, the values of the derivative are different. On the final nodes the values of the derivative equal the square of the price of copper. On other nodes they are calculated in the usual way. The current value of the security is $0.275 (see Figure 16.11).

117

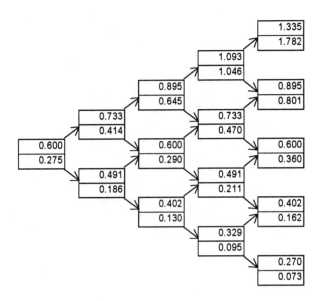

Figure 16.11   Tree to value derivative security in Problem 16.21. At each node, upper number is price of copper and lower number is derivative security price.

16.22. Define S_t as the current asset price, S_{max} as the highest asset price considered and S_{min} as the lowest asset price considered. (In the example in the text $S_{min} = 0$). Let

$$Q_1 = \frac{S_{max} - S_t}{\Delta S} \quad \text{and} \quad Q_2 = \frac{S_t - S_{min}}{\Delta S}$$

and let N be the number of time intervals considered. From the structure of the calculations in the explicit version of the finite difference method, it is easy to see that the values assumed for the derivative security at $S = S_{min}$ and $S = S_{max}$ affect the derivative security's value at time t if

$$N \geq \max(Q_1, Q_2)$$

16.23. A similar approach to that suggested for the binomial tree approach in Section 16.3 can be used. The grid can be used to model the stock price less the present value of future dividends during the life of the derivative security. This is the variable which is denoted by S^* in Section 16.3. It should be noted that, when this approach is used, the volatility which must be estimated is the volatility of S^* rather than the volatility of S. These two volatilities may be significantly different when a long-lived derivative security is being valued.

16.24. The basic approach is similar to that described in Section 16.8. The only difference is the boundary conditions. For a sufficiently small value of the stock price, S_{min}, it can be assumed that conversion will never take place and the convertible can be valued as a straight bond. The highest stock price which needs to be considered, $S_{\max}$, is $18. When this is reached the value of the convertible bond is $36. At maturity the convertible is worth the greater of $2S_T$ and $25 where S_T is the stock price.

The convertible can be valued by working backwards through the grid using either the explicit or the implicit finite difference method in conjunction with the boundary conditions. In formulas (16.25) and (16.32) the present value of the income on the convertible between time $t + i\,\Delta t$ and $t + (i+1)\,\Delta t$ discounted to time $t + i\,\Delta t$ must be added to the right-hand side. Chapter 23 considers the pricing of convertibles in more detail.

16.25. Suppose x_1, x_2, and x_3 are random samples from three independent normal distributions. Random samples with the required correlation structure are ϵ_1, ϵ_2, ϵ_3 where

$$\epsilon_1 = x_1$$

$$\epsilon_2 = \rho_{12}x_1 + x_2\sqrt{1 - \rho_{12}^2}$$

and

$$\epsilon_3 = \alpha_1 x_1 + \alpha_2 x_2 + \alpha_3 x_3$$

where

$$\alpha_1 = \rho_{13}$$

$$\alpha_1\rho_{12} + \alpha_2\sqrt{1 - \rho_{12}^2} = \rho_{23}$$

and

$$\alpha_1^2 + \alpha_2^2 + \alpha_3^2 = 1$$

This means that

$$\alpha_1 = \rho_{13}$$

$$\alpha_2 = \frac{\rho_{23} - \rho_{13}\rho_{12}}{\sqrt{1 - \rho_{12}^2}}$$

$$\alpha_3 = \sqrt{1 - \alpha_1^2 - \alpha_2^2}$$

CHAPTER 17
Volatility Smiles
and Alternatives to Black-Scholes

17.1. When both tails of the stock price distribution are thinner than those of the lognormal distribution, at-the-money options have higher implied volatilities than either in-the-money or out-of-the-money options. (This is the reverse of the situation in Figure 17.1 of the text.) When the right tail is fatter and the left tail is thinner, the implied volatility will be an increasing function of the strike price. (This is the reverse of the situation in Figure 17.3 of the text.)

17.2. When the stock price is positively correlated with volatility, we tend to get thin left tails and fat right tails. When the stock price increases, the volatility increases and much higher stock prices are then more likely than when volatility is constant. When the stock price decreases the volatility decreases and much lower stock prices are then less likely than when the volatility is constant. As in problem 17.1b, the implied volatility will be an increasing function of the strike price.

17.3. Jumps tend to make both tails of the stock price distribution fatter than those of the lognormal distribution. This means that we obtain the classic volatility smile shown in Figure 17.1 of the text. The volatility smile is more pronounced for three-month options than six-month options because, as pointed out in the text, the impact of jumps tends to disappear as we look further ahead.

17.4. The compound option model gives a stock price distribution with thinner right tails and fatter left tails than the lognormal distribution. The volatility smile is as in Figure 17.3 of the text. When Black–Scholes is used relatively high implied volatilities will be observed for in-the-money calls and out-of-the-money puts. Relatively low implied volatilities will be observed for out-of-the-money calls and in-the-money puts.

17.5. These biases are the same because of put–call parity. Suppose that p_{bs} and c_{bs} are the Black–Scholes prices of a European put and call, and that p_{mkt} and c_{mkt} are the put and call prices based in the market. Put–call parity must always be true. Hence with the usual notation

$$c_{bs} + Xe^{-rT} = p_{bs} + S$$

$$c_{mkt} + Xe^{-rT} = p_{mkt} + S$$

so that

$$c_{bs} - c_{mkt} = p_{bs} - p_{mkt}$$

showing that the bias for the call price is the same as the bias for the put price. When the call is in the money the put is out of the money and vice versa. This explains why the biases for in-the-money call options are usually the same as the biases for out-of-the-money put options.

17.6. The probability distribution of the stock price in one month is not lognormal. Possibly it consists of two lognormal distributions superimposed upon each other (one corresponding to a \$5 increase tomorrow; the other corresponding to a \$5 decrease tomorrow). Black–Scholes is clearly inappropriate since it assumes that the stock price at any future time is lognormal.

17.7. There are a number of problems in testing an option pricing model empirically. These include the problem of obtaining synchronous data on stock prices and option prices, the problem of estimating the dividends that will be paid on the stock during the option's life, the problem of distinguishing between situations where the market is inefficient and situations where the option pricing model is incorrect, and the problems of estimating stock price volatility.

17.8 (a) Suppose that S_1 is the stock price at time t_1 and S_T is the stock price at time T. From equation (11.1), it follows that in a risk- neutral world:

$$\ln S_1 - \ln S_0 \sim \phi \left[\left(r_1 - \frac{\sigma_1^2}{2} \right) t_1, \ \sigma_1 \sqrt{t_1} \right]$$

$$\ln S_T - \ln S_1 \sim \phi \left[\left(r_2 - \frac{\sigma_2^2}{2} \right) t_2, \ \sigma_2 \sqrt{t_2} \right]$$

Since the sum of two independent normal distributions is normal with mean equal to the sum of the means and variance equal to the sum of the variances

$$\ln S_T - \ln S_0 = (\ln S_T - \ln S_1) + (\ln S_1 - \ln S_0)$$

$$\sim \phi \left(r_1 t_1 + r_2 t_2 - \frac{\sigma_1^2 t_1}{2} - \frac{\sigma_2^2 t_2}{2}, \ \sqrt{\sigma_1^2 t_1 + \sigma_2^2 t_2} \right)$$

(b) Since:

$$r_1 t_1 + r_2 t_2 = \bar{r} T$$

and

$$\sigma_1^2 t_1 + \sigma_2^2 t_2 = \bar{V} T$$

it follows that:

$$\ln S_T - \ln S_0 \sim \phi \left[\left(\bar{r} - \frac{\bar{V}}{2} \right) T, \ \sqrt{\bar{V} T} \right]$$

(c) If σ_i and r_i are the volatility and risk-free interest rate during the ith subinterval ($i = 1, 2, 3$), an argument similar to that in (a) shows that:

$$\ln S_T - \ln S_0 \sim \phi \left(r_1 t_1 + r_2 t_2 + r_3 t_3 - \frac{\sigma_1^2 t_1}{2} - \frac{\sigma_2^2 t_2}{2} - \frac{\sigma_3^2 t_3}{2}, \ \sqrt{\sigma_1^2 t_1 + \sigma_2^2 t_2 + \sigma_3^2 t_3} \right)$$

where t_1, t_2 and t_3 are the lengths of the three subintervals. It follows that the result in (b) is still true.

(d) The result in (b) remains true as the time between time zero and time T is divided into more subintervals, each having its own risk-free interest rate and volatility. In the limit, it follows that, if r and σ are known functions of time, the stock price distribution at time T is the same as that for a stock with a constant interest rate and variance rate with the constant interest rate equal to the average interest rate and the constant variance rate equal to the average variance rate.

17.9. Suppose that there are N_1 voting shares and N_2 non-voting shares. Suppose further that P_1 and P_2 are the market prices of voting and non-voting shares respectively. Then:

$$P_1 = 1.1P_2$$

Define V as the total market value of the equity. It follows that:

$$
\begin{aligned}
V &= P_1 N_1 + P_2 N_2 \\
&= P_2(1.1N_1 + N_2) \\
&= P_1 \left(N_1 + \frac{N_2}{1.1} \right)
\end{aligned}
$$

P_1 is related to V by an equation of the form:

$$P_1 = aV$$

where a is constant. The volatility of V is constant. Suppose this is σ_V. The volatility of P_1 is also constant and equal to σ_V. It follows that the Black–Scholes formula is correct for valuing European options on the voting stock. (A similar argument shows that it is also correct for valuing European options on the non-voting stock.)

17.10. The volatilities would have the general form shown in Figure 17.1 in the text. Implied volatilities would be higher for deep-in and deep-out-of-the-money options than for at-the-money options. The volatility differences would be most noticeable for short-life options and gradually disappear as the option life increased. This is because jumps have a relatively greater impact on short maturity options.

17.11. When the stock price and volatility are negatively correlated, there is a volatility skew similar to that in Figure 17.3 of the text. This tends to become less pronounced as the life of the option increases.

17.12. In this case the probability distribution of the exchange rate has a thin left tail and a thin right tail relative to the lognormal distribution. We are in the opposite situation to that described for foreign currencies in section 17.2. Both out-of-the-money and in-the-money calls and puts can be expected to have lower implied volatilities than at-the-money calls and puts.

17.13 A deep-out-of-the-money option has a low value. Decreases in its volatility reduce its value. However, this reduction is small because the value can never go below zero. Increases in its volatility, on the other hand, can lead to significant percentage increases in the value of the option. The option does, therefore, have some of the same attributes as an option on volatility.

CHAPTER 18
Exotic Options

18.1. A forward start option is an option that is paid for now but will start at some time in the future. The strike price is usually equal to the price of the asset at the time the option starts. A chooser option is an option where, at some time in the future, the holder chooses whether the option is a call or a put.

18.2. A lookback call provides a payoff of $S_T - S_{\min}$. A lookback put provides a payoff of $S_{\max} - S_T$. A combination of a lookback call and a lookback put therefore provides a payoff of $S_{\max} - S_{\min}$.

18.3. No, it is never optimal to choose early. The resulting cash flows are the same regardless of when the choice is made. There is no point in the holder making a commitment earlier than necessary. This argument applies when the holder chooses between two American options providing the options cannot be exercised before the 2-year point. If the early exercise period starts as soon as the choice is made, the argument does not hold. For example, if the stock price fell to almost nothing in the first six months, the holder would choose a put option at this time and exercise it immediately.

18.4. The payoffs are as follows:
$c_1 : \max(\overline{S} - X, 0)$
$c_2 : \max(S_T - \overline{S}, 0)$
$c_3 : \max(S_T - X, 0)$
$p_1 : \max(X - \overline{S}, 0)$
$p_2 : \max(\overline{S} - S_T, 0)$
$p_3 : \max(X - S_T, 0)$
The payoff from $c_1 - p_1$ is always $\overline{S} - X$; The payoff from $c_2 - p_2$ is always $S_T - \overline{S}$; The payoff from $c_3 - p_3$ is always $S_T - X$; It follows that

$$c_1 - p_1 + c_2 - p_2 = c_3 - p_3$$

or

$$c_1 + c_2 - c_3 = p_1 + p_2 - p_3$$

18.5. Substituting for p, put-call parity gives

$$\max(c, p) = \max\left[p, \, p + S_1 e^{-q(T_2 - T_1)} - X e^{-r(T_2 - T_1)}\right]$$

$$= p + \max\left[0, \, S_1 e^{-q(T_2 - T_1)} - X e^{-r(T_2 - T_1)}\right]$$

124

This shows that the chooser option can be decomposed into
1. A put option with strike price X and maturity T_2; and
2. $e^{-q(T_2-T_1)}$ call options with strike price $Xe^{-(r-q)(T_2-T_1)}$ and maturity T_1.

18.6. Consider the formula for c_{do} when $H \geq X$

$$c_{\text{do}} = S_0 N(x_1)e^{-qT} - Xe^{-rT}N(x_1 - \sigma\sqrt{T}) - S_0 e^{-qT}(H/S_0)^{2\lambda}N(y_1)$$

$$+ Xe^{-rT}(H/S_0)^{2\lambda-2}N(y_1 - \sigma\sqrt{T})$$

Substituting $H = X$ and noting that

$$\lambda = \frac{r - q + \sigma^2/2}{\sigma^2}$$

we obtain $x_1 = d_1$ so that

$$c_{\text{do}} = c - S_0 e^{-qT}(H/S_0)^{2\lambda}N(y_1) + Xe^{-rT}(H/S_0)^{2\lambda-2}N(y_1 - \sigma\sqrt{T})$$

The formula for c_{di} when $H \leq X$ is

$$c_{\text{di}} = S_0 e^{-qT}(H/S_0)^{2\lambda}N(y) - Xe^{-rT}(H/S_0)^{2\lambda-2}N(y - \sigma\sqrt{T})$$

Since $c_{\text{do}} = c - c_{\text{di}}$

$$c_{\text{do}} = c - S_0 e^{-qT}(H/S_0)^{2\lambda}N(y) + Xe^{-rT}(H/S_0)^{2\lambda-2}N(y - \sigma\sqrt{T})$$

From the formulas in the text $y_1 = y$ when $H = X$. The two expression for c_{do} are therefore equivalent when $H = X$

18.7. The option is in the money only when the asset price is less than the strike price. However, in these circumstances the barrier has been hit and the option has ceased to exist.

18.8. In this case $S_0 = 1.6$, $r = 0.05$, $r_f = 0.08$, $\sigma = 0.15$, $T = 1.5$, $\Delta t = 0.5$. This means that

$$u = e^{0.15\sqrt{0.5}} = 1.1119$$

$$d = \frac{1}{u} = 0.8994$$

$$a = e^{(0.05-0.08)\times0.5} = 0.9851$$

$$p = \frac{a - d}{u - d} = 0.4033$$

$$1 - p = 0.5967$$

The option pays off

$$S_T - S_{\min}$$

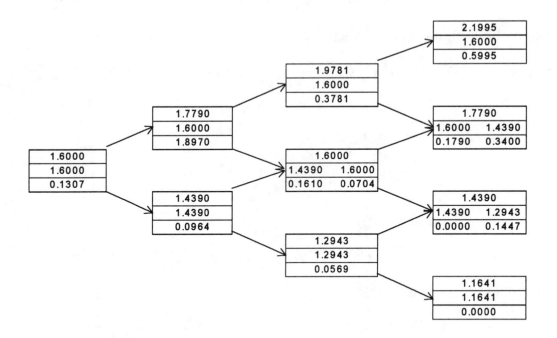

Figure 18.1   Binomial tree for Problem 18.8.

The tree is shown in Figure 18.1. At each node, the upper number is the exchange rate, the middle number(s) are the minimum exchange rate(s) so far, and the lower number(s) are the value(s) of the option. The tree shows that the value of the option today is 0.131.

18.9. In this case we construct a tree shown in Figure 18.2 for $Y(t) = F(t)/S(t)$ where $F(t)$ is the minimum value of the exchange rate to date and $S(t)$ is the current exchange rate. We use the tree to value the option in units of the foreign currency. That is we value an instrument that pays off $1 - Y(t)$. The tree shows that the value of the option is 0.0818 units of the foreign currency or $0.0818 \times 1.6 = 0.131$ units of the domestic currency. This is consistent with the answer to Problem 18.8.

18.10. In this case $S_0 = 40$, $X = 40$, $r = 0.1$, $\sigma = 0.35$, $T = 0.25$, $\Delta t = 0.08333$. This means that

$$u = e^{0.35\sqrt{0.08333}} = 1.1063$$

$$d = \frac{1}{u} = 0.9039$$

$$a = e^{0.1 \times 0.08333} = 1.008368$$

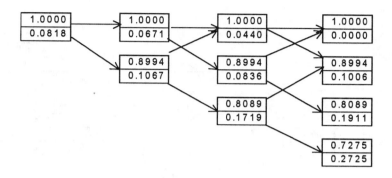

Figure 18.2   Tree for Problem 18.9.

$$p = \frac{a - d}{u - d} = 0.5161$$

$$1 - p = 0.4839$$

The option pays off

$$40 - \overline{S}$$

where $\overline{S}$ denotes the geometric average. The tree is shown in Figure 18.3. At each node, the upper number is the exchange rate, the middle number(s) are the geometric average(s), and the lower number(s) are the value(s) of the option. The geometric averages are calculated using the first, the last and all intermediate stock prices on the path. The tree shows that the value of the option today is $1.40.

18.11. The argument is similar to that given in Chapter 7 for a regular option on a non-dividend-paying stock. Consider a portfolio consisting of the option and cash equal to the present value of the terminal strike price. The initial cash position is

$$Xe^{gT - rT}$$

By time τ $(0 \leq \tau \leq T)$, the cash grows to

$$Xe^{-r(T-\tau)+gT} = Xe^{g\tau}e^{-(r-g)(T-\tau)}$$

Since $r > g$, this is less than $Xe^{g\tau}$ and therefore is less than the amount required to exercise the option. It follows that, if the option is exercised early, the terminal value of the portfolio is less than S_T. At time T the cash balance is Xe^{gT}. This is exactly what is required to exercise the option. If the early exercise decision is delayed until time T, the terminal value of the portfolio is therefore

$$\max[S_T, Xe^{gT}]$$

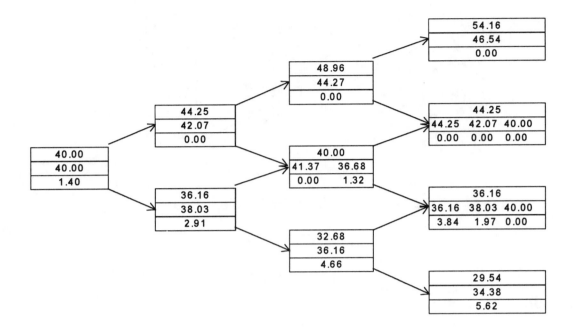

Figure 18.3   Binomial tree for Problem 18.10.

This is at least as great as S_T. It follows that early exercise cannot be optimal.

18.12. When the strike price of an option on a non-dividend-paying stock is defined as 10% greater that the stock price, the value of the option is proportional to the stock price. The same argument as that given in the text for forward start options shows that if t_1 is the time when the option starts and t_2 is the time when it finishes, the option has the same value as an option starting today with a life of $t_2 - t_1$ and a strike price of 1.1 times the current stock price.

18.13. Assume that we start calculating averages from time zero. The relationship between $A(t + \Delta t)$ and $A(t)$ is

$$A(t + \Delta t) \times (t + \Delta t) = A(t) \times t + S(t) \times \Delta t$$

where $S(t)$ is the stock price at time t and terms of higher order than Δt are ignored. If we continue to ignore terms of higher order than Δt, it follows that

$$A(t + \Delta t) = A(t) \left[1 - \frac{\Delta t}{t} \right] + S(t) \frac{\Delta t}{t}$$

Taking limits as Δt tends to zero

$$dA(t) = \frac{S(t) - A(t)}{t} dt$$

The process for $A(t)$ has a stochastic drift and no dz term. The process makes sense intuitively. Once time has passed, the change in S in the next small portion of time has only a second order effect on the average. If S equals A the average has no drift; if $S > A$ the average is drifting up; if $S < A$ the average is drifting down.

18.14. In an Asian option the payoff becomes more certain as time passes and the delta always approaches zero as the maturity date is approached. This makes delta hedging easy. Barrier options cause problems for delta hedgers when the asset price is close to the barrier because delta is discontinuous.

18.15. The value of the option is given by the formula in the text

$$S_2 e^{-q_2 T} N(d_1) - S_1 e^{-q_1 T} N(d_2)$$

where

$$d_1 = \frac{\ln(S_2/S_1) + (q_1 - q_2 + \sigma^2/2)T}{\sigma\sqrt{T}}$$

$$d_2 = d_1 - \sigma\sqrt{T}$$

and

$$\sigma = \sqrt{\sigma_1^2 + \sigma_2^2 - 2\rho\sigma_1\sigma_2}$$

In this case, $S_2 = 400$, $S_1 = 380$, $q_1 = 0$, $q_2 = 0$, $T = 1$, and

$$\sigma = \sqrt{0.2^2 + 0.2^2 - 2 \times 0.7 \times 0.2 \times 0.2} = 0.1549$$

Since $d_1 = 0.4086$ and $d_2 = 0.2536$, the option price is

$$400N(0.4086) - 380N(0.2536) = 35.4$$

or \$35.4.

18.16. No. If the future's price is above the spot price during the life of the option, it is possible that the spot price will hit the barrier when the futures price does not.

18.17. (a) The put–call relationship is

$$cc + X_1 e^{-rT_1} = pc + c$$

where cc is the price of the call on the call, pc is the price of the put on the call, c is the price today of the call into which the options can be exercised at time T_1, and X_1

is the exercise price for cc and pc. The proof is similar to that in Chapter 7 for the usual put–call parity relationship. Both sides of the equation represent the values of portfolios that will be worth $\max(c, X_1)$ at time T_1. From the formulas in the text, the relationships

$$M(a, b; \rho) = N(a) - M(a, -b; -\rho) = N(b) - M(-a, b, ; -\rho)$$

in Appendix 11C, and the relationship

$$N(x) = 1 - N(-x)$$

we obtain

$$cc - pc = Se^{-qT_2}N(b_1) - X_2e^{-rT_2}N(b_2) - X_1e^{-rT_1}$$

Since

$$c = Se^{-qT_2}N(b_1) - X_2e^{-rT_2}N(b_2)$$

put–call parity is consistent with the formulas
(b) The put–call relationship is

$$cp + X_1e^{-rT_1} = pp + p$$

where cp is the price of the call on the put, pp is the price of the put on the put, p is the price today of the put into which the options can be exercised at time T_1, and X_1 is the exercise price for cc and pc. The proof is similar to that in Chapter 7 for the usual put–call parity relationship. Both sides of the equation represent the values of portfolios that will be worth $\max(p, X_1)$ at time T_1. From the formulas in the text, the relationships

$$M(a, b; \rho) = N(a) - M(a, -b; -\rho) = N(b) - M(-a, b, ; -\rho)$$

in Appendix 11C, and the relationship

$$N(x) = 1 - N(-x)$$

it follows that

$$cp - pp = -Se^{-qT_2}N(-b_1) + X_2e^{-rT_2}N(-b_2) - X_1e^{-rT_1}$$

Since

$$p = -Se^{-qT_2}N(-b_1) - X_2e^{-rT_2}N(-b_2)$$

put–call parity is consistent with the formulas.

18.18. As we increase the frequency we observe a more extreme minimum which increases the value of a lookback call.

18.19. As we decrease the frequency with which the asset price is observed, the asset price becomes less likely to hit the barrier and the value of a down-and-out call goes up. For a similar reason the value of a down-and-in call goes down. The adjustment mentioned in the text, suggested by Broadie, Glasserman, and Kou, moves the barrier further out as the assset price is observed less frequently. This increases the price of a down-and-out option and reduces the price of a down-and-in option.

18.20. If the barrier is reached the down-and-out option is worth nothing while the down-and-in option has the same value as a regular option. If the barrier is not reached the down-and-in option is worth nothing while the down-and-out option has the same value as a regular option. This is why a down-and-out call option plus a down-and-in call option is worth the same as a regular option. A similar argument cannot be used for American options.

18.21. This is a cash-or-nothing call. The value is $100N(d_2)e^{-0.08 \times 0.5}$ where

$$d_2 = \frac{\ln(960/1000) + (0.08 - 0.03 - 0.2^2/2) \times 0.5}{0.2 \times \sqrt{0.5}} = -0.1826$$

Since $N(d_2) = 0.4276$ the value of the derivative is $41.08.

18.22. This is a regular call with a strike price of $20 that ceases to exist if the futures price hits $18. With the notation in the text $H = 18$, $X = 20$, $S = 19$, $r = 0.05$, $\sigma = 0.4$, $q = 0.05$, $T = 0.25$. From this $\lambda = 0.5$ and

$$y = \frac{\ln[18^2/(19 \times 20)]}{0.4\sqrt{0.25}} + 0.5 \times 0.4\sqrt{0.25} = -0.69714$$

The value of a down-and-out call plus a down-and-in call equals the value of a regular call. Substituting into the formula given when $H < X$ we get $c_{di} = 0.4638$. The regular Black–Scholes formula gives $c = 1.0902$. Hence $c_{do} = 0.6264$. (These answers can be checked with DerivaGem).

18.23. To use the approach in Section 18.4 we construct a tree for $Y(t) = F(t)/S(t)$ where $F(t)$ is the minimum value of the index to date and $S(t)$ is the value of the index at time t. The tree parameters are $a = 1.0050$, $p = 0.5000$, $u = 1.1052$, and $d = 0.9048$. We use the tree in Figure 18.4 to value the option in units of the stock index. This means that we value an instrument that pays off $1 - Y(t)$. The tree shows that the value of the option is 0.1019 units of the stock index or $400 \times 0.1019 = 40.47$ dollars. DerivaGem shows that the value given by the analytic formula is 53.38. This is higher than the value given by the tree because the tree assumes that the stock price is observed only three times when the minimum is calculated.

18.24. We can use the analytic approximation given in the text.

$$M_1 = \frac{(e^{0.05 \times 0.5} - 1) \times 30}{0.05 \times 0.5} = 30.378$$

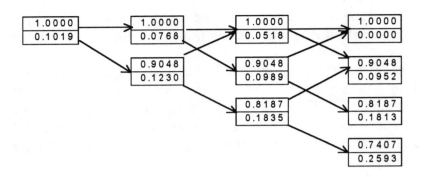

Figure 18.4 Tree for Problem 18.23.

Also $M_2 = 936.9$ so that $\sigma = 17.41\%$. The option can be valued as a futures option with $F_0 = 30.378$, $X = 30$, $r = 5\%$, $\sigma = 17.41\%$, and $t = 0.5$. The price is 1.637. (Note: there is a bug in the calculations of Asian option prices in version 1.2 of DerivaGem. A corrected version of the software can be downloaded from the author's web site.)

CHAPTER 19
Extensions of the Theoretical Framework for Pricing Derivatives: Martingales and Measures

19.1. The market price of risk for a variable that is not the price of a traded security is the market price of risk of a traded security whose price is instantaneously perfectly positively correlated with the variable.

19.2. If its market price of risk is zero, gold must, after storage costs have been paid, provide an expected return equal to the risk-free rate of interest. In this case, the expected return after storage costs must be 6% per annum. It follows that the expected growth rate in the price of gold must be 7% per annum.

This result can also be deduced from the equation in Section 19.3.

$$m - \lambda s = r - y + u$$

Since gold is an investment asset, $y = 0$. Also, $\lambda = 0$, $r = 0.06$, $u = 0.01$ so that $m = 0.07$ or 7% per annum.

19.3. Suppose that S is the security price and μ is the expected return from the security. Then:

$$\frac{dS}{S} = \mu dt + \sigma_1 dz_1 + \sigma_2 dz_2$$

where dz_1 and dz_2 are Wiener processes, $\sigma_1 dz_1$ is the component of the risk in the return attributable to the price of copper and $\sigma_2 dz_2$ is the component of the risk in the return attributable to the yen-$ exchange rate.
If the price of copper is held fixed, $dz_1 = 0$ and:

$$\frac{dS}{S} = \mu dt + \sigma_2 dz_2$$

Hence σ_2 is 8% per annum or 0.08. If the yen-$ exchange rate is held fixed, $dz_2 = 0$ and:

$$\frac{dS}{S} = \mu dt + \sigma_1 dz_1$$

Hence σ_1 is 12% per annum or 0.12.
From equation (19.13)

$$\mu - r = \lambda_1 \sigma_1 + \lambda_2 \sigma_2$$

where λ_1 and λ_2 are the market prices of risk for copper and the yen-$ exchange rate. In this case, $r = 0.07$, $\lambda_1 = 0.5$ and $\lambda_2 = 0.1$. Therefore

$$\mu - 0.07 = 0.5 \times 0.12 + 0.1 \times 0.08$$

so that

$$\mu = 0.138$$

i.e., the expected return is 19.8% per annum.

If the two variables affecting S are uncorrelated, we can use the result that the sum of normally distributed variables is normal with variance of the sum equal to the sum of the variances. This leads to:

$$\sigma_1 dz_1 + \sigma_2 dz_2 = \sqrt{\sigma_1^2 + \sigma_2^2} dz_3$$

where dz_3 is a Wiener process. Hence the process for S becomes:

$$\frac{dS}{S} = \mu dt + \sqrt{\sigma_1^2 + \sigma_2^2} dz_3$$

If follows that the volatility of S is $\sqrt{\sigma_1^2 + \sigma_2^2}$ or 14.4% per annum.

19.4. It can be argued that the market price of risk for the second variable is zero. This is because the risk is unsystematic, i.e., it is totally unrelated to other risks in the economy. To put this another way, there is no reason why investors should demand a higher return for bearing the risk since the risk can be totally diversified away.

19.5. Suppose that the price, f, of the derivative depends on the prices, S_1 and S_2, of two traded securities. Suppose further that:

$$dS_1 = \mu_1 S_1 dt + \sigma_1 S_1 dz_1$$

$$dS_2 = \mu_2 S_2 dt + \sigma_2 S_2 dz_2$$

where dz_1 and dz_2 are Wiener processes with correlation ρ. From Ito's lemma [see equation (19A.3)]

$$df = \left(\mu_1 S_1 \frac{\partial f}{\partial S_1} + \mu_2 S_2 \frac{\partial f}{\partial S_2} + \frac{\partial f}{\partial t} + \frac{1}{2} \sigma_1^2 \frac{\partial^2 f}{\partial S_1^2} + \frac{1}{2} \sigma_2^2 \frac{\partial^2 f}{\partial S_2^2} \right.$$
$$\left. + \rho \sigma_1 \sigma_2 \frac{\partial^2 f}{\partial S_1 \partial S_2} \right) dt + \sigma_1 S_1 \frac{\partial f}{\partial S_1} dz_1 + \sigma_2 S_2 \frac{\partial f}{\partial S_2} dz_2$$

To eliminate the dz_1 and dz_2 we choose a portfolio, Π, consisting of

$$\begin{array}{ll} -1: & \text{derivative} \\ +\frac{\partial f}{\partial S_1}: & \text{first traded security} \\ +\frac{\partial f}{\partial S_2}: & \text{second traded security} \end{array}$$

134

$$\Pi = -f + \frac{\partial f}{\partial S_1}S_1 + \frac{\partial f}{\partial S_2}S_2$$

$$d\Pi = -df + \frac{\partial f}{\partial S_1}dS_1 + \frac{\partial f}{\partial S_2}dS_2$$

$$= -\left(\frac{\partial f}{\partial t} + \frac{1}{2}\sigma_1^2\frac{\partial^2 f}{\partial S_1^2} + \frac{1}{2}\sigma_2^2\frac{\partial^2 f}{\partial S_2^2} + \rho\sigma_1\sigma_2\frac{\partial^2 f}{\partial S_1\partial S_2}\right)dt$$

Since the portfolio is instantaneously risk-free it must instantaneously earn the risk-free rate of interest. Hence

$$d\Pi = r\Pi dt$$

Combining the above equations

$$-\left[\frac{\partial f}{\partial t} + \frac{1}{2}\sigma_1^2\frac{\partial^2 f}{\partial S_1^2} + \frac{1}{2}\sigma_2^2\frac{\partial^2 f}{\partial S_2^2} + \rho\sigma_1\sigma_2\frac{\partial^2 f}{\partial S_1\partial S_2}\right]dt = r\left[-f + \frac{\partial f}{\partial S_1}S_1 + \frac{\partial f}{\partial S_2}S_2\right]dt$$

so that:

$$\frac{\partial f}{\partial t} + rS_1\frac{\partial f}{\partial S_1} + rS_2\frac{\partial f}{\partial S_2} + \frac{1}{2}\sigma_1^2\frac{\partial^2 f}{\partial S_1^2} + \frac{1}{2}\sigma_2^2\frac{\partial^2 f}{\partial S_2^2} + \rho\sigma_1\sigma_2\frac{\partial^2 f}{\partial S_1\partial S_2} = rf$$

This corresponds to equation (19B.11) since $m_1 - \lambda_1\sigma_1 = m_2 - \lambda_2\sigma_2 = r$. Note that it has not been necessary to bring market prices of risk into the analysis as both underlying variables are traded securities.

19.6. From Section 19.3

$$y = r + u - m + \lambda s$$

In this case $y = 0.05$, $u = 0.01$, $r = 0.06$, $m = 0$. It follows that

$$\lambda s = 0.05 - 0.06 - 0.01 = -0.02$$

From risk-neutral valuation arguments

$$\hat{E}(S_T) = S_0 e^{(m-\lambda s)T}$$

Since

$$F = \hat{E}(S_T)$$

$$F = S_0 e^{(m-\lambda s)T}$$

It is also true that

$$E(S_T) = S_0 e^{mT}$$

It follows that

$$F = E(S_T)e^{-\lambda s T}$$

In this case:
$$F = E(S_T)e^{0.02 \times 0.5}$$
$$= 1.01 \, E(S_T)$$

The six months' futures price is therefore 1% higher than the expected future spot price in six months' time.

19.7. From Problem 19.6
$$F = E(S_T)e^{-\lambda s T}$$

In this case $\lambda = 0.5$, $s = 0.2$, $S = 0.80$, $F = 0.75$ and $T = 0.50$.
$$F = E(S_T)e^{-\lambda\sigma(T-t)}$$
$$E(S_T) = 0.75e^{0.5 \times 0.2 \times 0.5}$$
$$= 0.7885$$

Since it is also true that
$$E(S_T) = S_0 e^{mT}$$
$$0.7885 = 0.80 e^{m \times 0.50}$$

or
$$m = \frac{1}{0.50} \ln \frac{0.7885}{0.80}$$
$$= -0.030$$

The expected growth rate is -3% per annum.

19.8. The process for x can be written
$$\frac{dx}{x} = \frac{a(x_0 - x)}{x} dt + \frac{c}{\sqrt{x}} dz$$

Hence the expected growth rate in x is:
$$\frac{a(x_0 - x)}{x}$$

and the volatility of x is
$$\frac{c}{\sqrt{x}}$$

In a risk neutral world the expected growth rate should be changed to
$$\frac{a(x_0 - x)}{x} - \lambda \frac{c}{\sqrt{x}}$$

so that the process is
$$\frac{dx}{x} = \left[\frac{a(x_0 - x)}{x} - \lambda \frac{c}{\sqrt{x}} \right] dt + \frac{c}{\sqrt{x}} dz$$

i.e.

$$dx = \left[a(x_0 - x) - \lambda c\sqrt{x}\right]dt + c\sqrt{x}dz$$

Hence the drift rate should be reduced by $\lambda c\sqrt{x}$.

19.9. As suggested in the hint we form a new security f^* which is the same as f except that all income produced by f is reinvested in f. Assuming we start doing this at time zero, the relationship between f and f^* is

$$f^* = fe^{qt}$$

$$\frac{df^*}{f^*} = \frac{df}{f} + q$$

If μ^* and σ^* is the expected return and volatility of f^* this equation shows that

$$\mu^* = \mu + q$$

$$\sigma^* = \sigma$$

From equation (19.8) or

$$\frac{\mu + q - r}{\sigma} = \lambda$$

and substituting from Ito's lemma for μ and σ equation (19.10) becomes

$$\frac{\partial f^*}{\partial t} + \theta\frac{\partial f^*}{\partial \theta}(m - \lambda s) + \frac{1}{2}s^2\theta^2\frac{\partial^2 f^*}{\partial \theta^2} = rf^*$$

Substituting $f^* = fe^{qt}$

$$\frac{\partial f}{\partial t} + \theta\frac{\partial f}{\partial \theta}(m - \lambda s) + \frac{1}{2}s^2\theta^2\frac{\partial^2 f}{\partial \theta^2} = (r - q)f$$

Risk-neutral valuation shows that we can value f by reducing the drift in θ from m to $m - \lambda s$ and then discounting at $r - q$

19.10. As suggested in the hint, we form two new securities f^* and g^* which are the same as f and g at time zero, but are such that income from f is reinvested in f and income from g is reinvested in g. By construction f^* and g^* are non-income producing and their values at time t are related to f and g by

$$f^* = fe^{q_f t} \qquad g^* = ge^{q_g t}$$

From Ito's lemma, the securities g and g^* have the same volatility. We can apply the analysis given in Section 19.4 to f^* and g^* so that from equation (19.19)

$$f_0^* = g_0^* E_g\left(\frac{f_T^*}{g_T^*}\right)$$

137

or

$$f_0 = g_0 E_g \left(\frac{f_T e^{q_f T}}{g_T e^{q_g T}} \right)$$

or

$$f_0 = g_0 e^{(q_f - q_g)T} E_g \left(\frac{f_T}{g_T} \right)$$

19.11. In this case

$$\frac{dS}{S} = \mu(t)\, dt + \sigma\, dz$$

or

$$d\ln S = [\mu(t) - \sigma^2/2]\, dt + \sigma\, dz$$

so that $\ln S_T$ is normal with mean

$$\ln S_0 + \int_{t=0}^{T} \mu(t) dt - \sigma^2 T/2$$

and standard deviation $\sigma\sqrt{T}$. Section 19.3 shows that

$$\mu(t) = \frac{\partial}{\partial t}[\ln F(t)]$$

so that

$$\int_{t=0}^{T} \mu(t) dt = \ln F(T) - \ln F(0)$$

Since $F(0) = S_0$ the result follows.

19.12. The interest rate must have a negative market price of risk. Since bond prices and interest rates are negatively correlated, the statement implies that the market price of risk for a bond price is positive. The statement is reasonable. When interest rates increase, there is a tendency for the stock market to decrease. This implies that interest rates have negative systematic risk, or equivalently that bond prices have positive systematic risk.

19.13. (a) In the traditional risk-neutral world the process followed by S is

$$dS = (r - q)S\, dt + \sigma_S S\, dz$$

where r is the instantaneous risk-free rate. The market price of dz-risk is zero.
(b) In the traditional risk-neutral world for currency B the process is

$$dS = (r - q + \rho_{Q,S}\sigma_S\sigma_Q)S\, dt + \sigma_S S\, dz$$

where Q is the exchange rate (units of A per unit of B), σ_Q is the volatility of Q and $\rho_{Q,S}$ is the coefficient of correlation between Q and S. The market price of dz-risk is $\rho_{Q,S}\sigma_Q$

(c) In a world that is forward risk neutral with respect to a zero-coupon bond in currency A maturing at time T

$$dS = (r - q + \sigma_S\sigma_P)S\,dt + \sigma_S S\,dz$$

where σ_P is the bond price volatility. The market price of dz-risk is σ_P

(d) In a world that is forward risk neutral with respect to a zero-coupon bond in currency B maturing at time T

$$dS = (r - q + \sigma_S\sigma_P + \rho_{F,S}\sigma_S\sigma_F)S\,dt + \sigma_S S\,dz$$

where F is the forward exchange rate, σ_F is the volatility of F (units of A per unit of B, and $\rho_{F,S}$ is the correlation between F and S. The market price of dz-risk is $\sigma_A + \rho_{F,S}\sigma_F$.

19.14. Define

$P(t, T)$: Price in yen at time t of a bond paying 1 yen at time T

$E_T(\cdot)$: Expectation in world that is forward risk neutral with respect to $P(t, T)$

$\qquad F$: Dollar forward price of gold for a contract maturing at time T

$\qquad F_0$: Value of F at time zero

$\qquad \sigma_F$: Volatility of F

$\qquad G$: Forward exchange rate (dollars per yen)

$\qquad \sigma_G$: Volatility of G

We assume that S_T is lognormal. We can work in a world that is forward risk neutral with respect to $P(t, T)$ to get the value of the call as

$$P(0, T)[E_T(S_T)N(d_1) - XN(d_2)]$$

where

$$d_1 = \frac{\ln[E_T(S_T)/X] + \sigma_F^2 T/2}{\sigma_F\sqrt{T}}$$

$$d_2 = \frac{\ln[E_T(S_T)/X] - \sigma_F^2 T/2}{\sigma_F\sqrt{T}}$$

From section 19.9

$$E_T(S_T) = F_0 e^{\rho\sigma_F\sigma_G T}$$

Hence the option price, measured in yen, is

$$P(0, T)[F_0 e^{\rho\sigma_F\sigma_G T}N(d_1) - XN(d_2)]$$

where

$$d_1 = \frac{\ln[F_0 e^{\rho\sigma_F\sigma_G T}/X] + \sigma_F^2 T/2}{\sigma_F\sqrt{T}}$$

$$d_2 = \frac{\ln[F_0 e^{\rho\sigma_F\sigma_G T}/X] - \sigma_F^2 T/2}{\sigma_F\sqrt{T}}$$

19.15 (a) The value of the option can be calculated by setting $S_0 = 400$, $X = 400$, $r = 0.06$, $q = 0.02$, $\sigma = 0.2$, and $T = 2$. With 100 time steps the value (in Canadian dollars) is 57.87.

(b) In this case we increase the growth rate of the index by $0.4 \times 0.2 \times 0.06$ or 0.48% per year. This is equivalent to reducing the dividend yield to 1.52%. We therefore value the option by setting $S_0 = 400$, $X = 400$, $r = 0.06$, $q = 0.0152$, $\sigma = 0.2$, and $T = 2$. With 100 time steps the value (in U.S. dollars) is 60.35.

CHAPTER 20
Interest Rate Derivatives:
The Standard Market Models

20.1. An amount

$$\$20,000,000 \times 0.02 \times 0.25 = \$100,000$$

would be paid out 3 months later.

20.2. A swaption is an option to enter into an interest rate swap at a certain time in the future with a certain fixed rate being used. An interest rate swap can be regarded as the exchange of a fixed-rate bond for a floating-rate bond. A swaption is therefore the option to exchange a fixed-rate bond for a floating-rate bond. The floating-rate bond will be worth its face value at the beginning of the life of the swap. The swaption is therefore an option on a fixed-rate bond with the strike price equal to the face value of the bond.

20.3 In this case, $F_0 = (125 - 10)e^{0.1 \times 1} = 127.09$, $X = 110$, $r = 0.1$, $\sigma = 0.08$, and $T = 1.0$.

$$d_1 = \frac{\ln(127.09/110) + (0.08^2/2)}{0.08} = 1.8456$$
$$d_2 = d_1 - 0.08 = 1.7656$$

The value of the put option is

$$110e^{-0.1}N(-1.7656) - 115N(-1.8456) = 0.12$$

or \$0.12.

20.4. Suppose that the fixed rate accrues only when the floating reference rate is below R_X and above R_Y where $R_Y < R_X$. In this case the swap is a regular swap plus two series of binary options, one for each day of the life of the swap. Using the notation in the text, the risk-neutral probability that LIBOR will be above R_X on day i is $N(d_2)$ where

$$d_2 = \frac{\ln(F_i/R_X) - \sigma_i^2 t_i^2/2}{\sigma_i \sqrt{t_i}}$$

The probability that it will be below R_Y where $R_Y < R_X$ is $N(-d_2^*)$ where

$$d_2^* = \frac{\ln(F_i/R_Y) - \sigma_i^2 t_i^2/2}{\sigma_i \sqrt{t_i}}$$

From the viewpoint of the party paying fixed, the swap is a regular swap plus binary options. The binary options corresponding to day i have a total value of

$$\frac{QL}{n_2} P(0, s_i)[N(d_2) + N(-d_2^*)]$$

(This ignores the small timing adjustment mentioned in the text.)

20.5. (a) A convexity adjustment is necessary for the swap rate
(b) No convexity or timing adjustments are necessary.

20.6. When spot volatilities are used to value a cap, a different volatility is used to value each caplet. When flat volatilities are used, the same volatility is used to value each caplet within a given cap. Spot volatilities are a function of the maturity of the caplet. Flat volatilities are a function of the maturity of the cap.

20.7. In this case $L = 1000$, $\delta_k = 0.25$, $F_k = 0.12$, $R_X = 0.13$, $r = 0.115$, $\sigma_k = 0.12$, $t_k = 1.25$, $P(0, t_{k+1}) = 0.8416$.

$$L\delta_k = 250$$

$$d_1 = \frac{\ln(0.12/0.13) + 0.12^2 \times 1.25/2}{0.12\sqrt{1.25}} = -0.5295$$

$$d_2 = -0.5295 - 0.12\sqrt{1.25} = -0.6637$$

The value of the option is

$$250 \times 0.8416 \times [0.12N(-0.5295) - 0.13N(-0.6637)]$$

$$= 0.59$$

or $0.59.

20.8. The implied volatility measures the standard deviation of the logarithm of the bond price at the maturity of the option divided by the square root of the time to maturity. In the case of a five year option on a ten year bond, the bond has five years left at option maturity. In the case of a nine year option on a ten year bond it has one year left. The standard deviation of a one year bond price observed in nine years can be normally be expected to be considerably less than that of a five year bond price observed in five years. (See Figure 20.1.) We would therefore expect the price to be too high.

20.9. The present value of the principal in the four year bond is $100e^{-4\times0.1} = 67.032$. The present value of the coupons is, therefore, $102 - 67.032 = 34.968$. This means that the forward price of the five-year bond is

$$(105 - 34.968)e^{4\times0.1} = 104.475$$

The parameters in Black's model are therefore $F_0 = 104.475$, $X = 100$, $r = 0.1$, $T = 4$, and $\sigma = 0.02$.

$$d_1 = \frac{\ln 1.04475 + 0.5 \times 0.02^2 \times 4}{0.02\sqrt{4}} = 1.1144$$

$$d_2 = d_1 - 0.02\sqrt{4} = 1.0744$$

The price of the European call is

$$e^{-0.1 \times 4}[104.475N(1.1144) - 100N(1.0744)] = 3.19$$

or \$3.19.

20.10. A 5-year zero-cost collar where the strike price of the cap equals the strike price of the floor is the same as an interest rate swap agreement to receive floating and pay a fixed rate equal to the strike price. The common strike price is the swap rate. Note that the swap is actually a forward swap that excludes the first exchange. (See footnote 3 of chapter 20.)

20.11. There are two way of expressing the put–call parity relationship for bond options. The first is in terms of bond prices:

$$c + I + Xe^{-RT} = p + B$$

where c is the price of a European call option, p is the price of the corresponding European put option, I is the present value of the bond coupon payments during the life of the option, X is the strike price, T is the time to maturity, B is the bond price, and R is the risk-free interest rate for a maturity equal to the life of the options. To prove this we can consider two portfolios. The first consists of a European put option plus the bond; the second consists of the European call option, and an amount of cash equal to the present value of the coupons plus the present value of the strike price. Both can be seen to be worth the same at the maturity of the options.

The second way of expressing the put–call parity relationship is

$$c + Xe^{-RT} = p + F_0 e^{-RT}$$

where F_0 is the forward bond price. This can also be proved by considering two portfolios. The first consists of a European put option plus a forward contract on the bond plus the present value of the forward price; the second consists of a European call option plus the present value of the strike price. Both can be seen to be worth the same at the maturity of the options.

20.12. The put–call parity relationship for European swap options is

$$c + V = p$$

where c is the value of a call option to pay a fixed rate of R_X and receive floating, p is the value of a put option to receive a fixed rate of R_X and pay floating, and V is the value of the forward swap underlying the swap option where R_X is received and floating is paid. This can be proved by considering two portfolios. The first consists of the put option; the second consists of the call option and the swap. Suppose that the actual swap rate at the maturity of the options is greater than R_X. The call will be exercised and the put will not be exercised. Both portfolios are then worth zero. Suppose next that the actual swap rate at the maturity of the options is less than R_X. The put option is exercised and the call option is not exercised. Both portfolios are equivalent to a swap where R_X is received and floating is paid. In all states of the world the two portfolios are worth the same at time T. They must therefore be worth the same today. This proves the result.

20.13. Suppose that the cap and floor have the same strike price and the same time to maturity. The following put–call parity relationship must hold:

$$\text{cap} + \text{swap} = \text{floor}$$

where the swap is an agreement to receive the cap rate and pay floating over the whole life of the cap/floor. If the implied Black volatilities for the cap equals that for the floor, the Black formulas show that this relationship holds. In other circumstances it does not hold and there is an arbitrage opportunity. The broker quotes in Table 20.1 do not present an arbitrage opportunity because the cap offer is always higher than the floor bid and the floor offer is always higher than the cap bid.

20.14. Yes. If a discount bond price at some future time is lognormal, there is some chance that the price will be above par. This in turn implies that the yield to maturity on the bond is negative.

20.15. There are two differences. The discounting is done over a 1.0-year period instead of over a 1.25-year period. Also a convexity adjustment to the forward rate is necessary. To calculate the convexity adjustment we define $G(y)$ as the price at time 1 year of a three-month bond as a function of the quarterly compounded three-month rate at that time.

$$G(y) = \frac{1}{1 + 0.25y}$$

$$G'(y) = -\frac{0.25}{(1 + 0.25y)^2}$$

$$G''(y) = \frac{0.125}{(1 + 0.25y)^3}$$

Since $F = 0.07$, $G'(F) = -0.2415$ and $G''(F) = 0.1187$. The convexity adjustment is therefore

$$0.5 \times 0.07^2 \times 0.2^2 \times 1 \times \frac{0.1187}{0.2415} = 0.00005$$

or about half a basis point.

In the formula for the caplet we set $F_k = 0.07005$ instead of 0.07. This means that $d_1 = -0.5642$ and $d_2 = -0.7642$. With continuous compounding the 15-month rate is 6.5% and the forward rate between 12 and 15 months is 6.94%. The 12 month rate is therefore 6.39% The caplet price becomes

$$0.25 \times 10,000e^{-0.0639 \times 1.0}[0.07005N(-0.5642) - 0.08N(-0.7642)] = 5.31$$

or $5.31.

20.16 The convexity adjustment discussed in Section 20.11 leads to the instrument being worth an amount slightly different from zero. Define $G(y)$ as the value as seen in five years of a two-year bond with a coupon of 10% as a function of its yield.

$$G(y) = \frac{0.1}{1+y} + \frac{1.1}{(1+y)^2}$$

$$G'(y) = -\frac{0.1}{(1+y)^2} - \frac{2.2}{(1+y)^3}$$

$$G''(y) = \frac{0.2}{(1+y)^3} + \frac{6.6}{(1+y)^4}$$

It follows that $G'(0.1) = -1.7355$ and $G''(0.1) = 4.6582$ and the convexity adjustment that must be made for the two-year swap- rate is

$$0.5 \times 0.1^2 \times 0.2^2 \times 5 \times \frac{4.6582}{1.7355} = 0.00268$$

We can therefore value the instrument on the assumption that the swap rate will be 10.268% in five years. The value of the instrument is

$$\frac{0.268}{1.1^5} = 0.167$$

or $0.167.

20.17. In this case we have to make a timing adjustment as well as a convexity adjustment to the forward swap rate. For (a) equation (20.18) shows that the timing adjustment involves multiplying the swap rate by

$$\exp\left[-\frac{0.8 \times 0.20 \times 0.20 \times 0.1 \times 5}{1 + 0.1}\right] = 0.9856$$

so that it becomes $10.268 \times 0.9856 = 10.120$. The value of the instrument is

$$\frac{0.120}{1.1^5} = 0.075$$

or $0.075.

145

For (b) equation (20.18) shows that the timing adjustment involves multiplying the swap rate by

$$\exp\left[-\frac{0.95 \times 0.2 \times 0.2 \times 0.1 \times 2 \times 5}{1 + 0.1}\right] = 0.9627$$

so that it becomes $10.268 \times 0.9627 = 9.885$. The value of the instrument is now

$$-\frac{0.115}{1.1^5} == 0.086$$

or −$0.086.

20.18. In equation (20.14), $L = 10,000,000$, $R_X = 0.05$, $F_0 = 0.05$, $d_1 = 0.2\sqrt{4}/2 = 0.2$, $d_2 = -.2$, and

$$A = \frac{1}{1.055^5} + \frac{1}{1.055^6} + \frac{1}{1.055^7} = 2.2404$$

The value of the swap (in millions of dollars) is

$$10 \times 2.2404[0.05N(0.2) - 0.05N(-0.2)] = 0.178$$

This is the same as the answer given by DerivaGem. (For the purposes of using the DerivaGem software note that the interest rate is 4.879% with continuous compounding for all maturities.)

20.19. The price of the bond at time t is $e^{-R(T-t)}$ where T is the time when the bond matures. Using Ito's lemma the volatility of the bond price is

$$\sigma\frac{\partial}{\partial R}e^{-R(T-t)} = -\sigma(T-t)e^{-R(T-t)}$$

This tends to zero as t approaches T.

20.20. (a) The process for y is
$$dy = \alpha y\, dt + \sigma_y y\, dz$$

The forward bond price is $G(y)$. From Ito's lemma, its process is

$$d[G(y)] = [G'(y)\alpha y + \frac{1}{2}G''(y)\sigma_y^2 y^2]\, dt + G'(y)\sigma_y y\, dz$$

(b) Since the expected growth rate of $G(y)$ is zero

$$G'(y)\alpha y + \frac{1}{2}G''(y)\sigma_y^2 y^2 = 0$$

or

$$\alpha = -\frac{1}{2}\frac{G''(y)}{G'(y)}\sigma_y^2 y$$

146

(c) Assuming as an approximation that y always equals its initial value of y_0, this shows that the growth rate of y is

$$-\frac{1}{2}\frac{G''(y_0)}{G'(y_0)}\sigma_y^2 y_0$$

The variable y starts at y_0 and ends as y_T. The convexity adjustment to y_0 when we are calculating the expected value of y_T in a world that is forward risk neutral with respect to a zero-coupon bond maturing at time T is approximately $y_0 T$ times this or

$$-\frac{1}{2}\frac{G''(y_0)}{G'(y_0)}\sigma_y^2 y_0^2 T$$

This is consistent with equation (20.15).

CHAPTER 21
Interest Rate Derivatives: Models of the Short Rate

21.1. Equilibrium models usually start with assumptions about economic variables and derive the behavior of interest rates. The initial term structure is an output from the model. In a no-arbitrage model the initial term structure is an input. The behavior of interest rates in a no-arbitrage model is designed to be consistent with the initial term structure.

21.2. If the price of a traded security followed a mean-reverting or path-dependent process there would be a market inefficiency. The short-term interest rate is not the price of a traded security. In other words we cannot trade something whose price is always the short-term interest rate. There is therefore no market inefficiency when the short-term interest rate follows a mean-reverting or path-dependent process. We can trade bonds and other instruments whose prices do depend on the short rate. The prices of these instruments do not follow mean-reverting or path-dependent processes.

21.3. In Vasicek's model the standard deviation stays at 1%. In the Rendleman and Bartter model the standard deviation is proportional to the level of the short rate. When the short rate increases from 4% to 8% the standard deviation increases from 1% to 2%. In the Cox, Ingersoll, and Ross model the standard deviation of the short rate is proportional to the square root of the short rate. When the short rate increases from 4% to 8% the standard deviation of the short rate increases from 1% to 1.414%.

21.4. In a one-factor model there is one source of uncertainty driving all rates. This usually means that in any short period of time all rates move in the same direction (but not necessarily by the same amount). In a two-factor model, there are two sources of uncertainty driving all rates. The first source of uncertainty usually gives rise to a roughly parallel shift in rates. The second gives rise to a twist where long and short rates moves in opposite directions.

21.5. No. The approach in section 21.4 relies on the argument that, at any given time, all bond prices are moving in the same direction. This is not true when there is more than one factor.

21.6. In Vasicek's model, $a = 0.1$, $b = 0.1$, and $\sigma = 0.02$ so that

$$B(t, t+10) = \frac{1}{0.1}(1 - e^{-0.1 \times 10}) = 6.32121$$

$$A(t, t+10) = \exp\left[\frac{(6.32121 - 10)(0.1^2 \times 0.1 - 0.0002)}{0.01} - \frac{0.0004 \times 6.32121^2}{0.4}\right]$$

$$= 0.71587$$

The bond price is therefore $0.71587e^{-6.32121\times0.1} = 0.38046$

In the Cox, Ingersoll, and Ross model, $a = 0.1$, $b = 0.1$ and $\sigma = 0.02/\sqrt{0.1} = 0.0632$. Also

$$\gamma = \sqrt{a^2 + 2\sigma^2} = 0.13416$$

Define

$$\beta = (\gamma + a)(e^{10\gamma} - 1) + 2\gamma = 0.92992$$

$$B(t, t+10) = \frac{2(e^{10\gamma} - 1)}{\beta} = 6.07650$$

$$A(t, t+10) = \left(\frac{2\gamma e^{5(a+\gamma)}}{\beta}\right)^{2ab/\sigma^2} = 0.69746$$

The bond price is therefore $0.69746e^{-6.07650\times0.1} = 0.37986$

21.7. Using the notation in the text $s = 3$, $T = 1$, $L = 100$, $X = 87$,

$$\sigma_P = \frac{0.015}{0.1}(1 - e^{-2\times0.1})\sqrt{\frac{1 - e^{-2\times0.1\times1}}{2 \times 0.1}} = 0.025886$$

Also using the formulas in the text $P(0, 1) = 0.94988$, $P(0, 3) = 0.85092$, and $h = 1.14277$ so that the call price is

$$100 \times 0.85092 \times N(1.14277) - 87 \times 0.94988 \times N(1.11688) = 2.59$$

or \$2.59.

21.8. The put price is

$$87 \times 0.94988 \times N(-1.11688) - 100 \times 0.85092 \times N(-1.14277) = 0.14$$

Since the underlying bond pays no coupon, put–call parity states that the put price plus the bond price should equal the call price plus the present value of the strike price. The bond price is 85.09 and the present value of the strike price is $87 \times 0.94988 = 82.64$. Put–call parity is therefore satisfied:

$$82.64 + 2.59 = 85.09 + 0.14$$

21.9. The first stage is to calculate the value of r at time 2.1 years which is such that the value of the bond at that time is 99. Denoting this value of r by r^*, we must solve

$$2.5A(2.1, 2.5)e^{-B(2.1,2.5)r^*} + 102.5A(2.1, 3.0)e^{-B(2.1,3.0)r^*} = 99$$

The solution to this is $r^* = 0.063$. Since

$$2.5A(2.1, 2.5)e^{-B(2.1, 2.5) \times 0.063} = 2.43624$$

and

$$102.5A(2.1, 3.0)e^{-B(2.1, 3.0) \times 0.063} = 96.56373$$

the call option on the coupon-bearing bond can be decomposed into a call option with a strike price of 2.43624 on a bond that pays off 2.5 at time 2.5 years and a call option with a strike price of 96.56373 on a bond that pays off 102.5 at time 3.0 years. The formulas in the text show that the value of the first option is 0.0015 and the value of the second option is 0.1229. The total value of the option is therefore 0.1244.

21.10. Put-call parity shows that:

$$c + I + PV(X) = p + B_0$$

or

$$p = c + PV(X) - (B_0 - I)$$

where c is the call price, X is the strike price, I is the present value of the coupons, and B_0 is the bond price. In this case $c = 0.1244$, $PV(X) = 99 \times P(0, 2.1) = 85.9093$, $B_0 - I = 2.5 \times P(0, 2.5) + 102.5 \times P(0, 3) = 85.3124$ so that the put price is

$$0.1244 + 85.9093 - 85.3124 = 0.7213$$

21.11. Using the notation in the text $P(0, T) = e^{-0.1 \times 1} = 0.9048$ and $P(0, s) = e^{-0.1 \times 5} = 0.6065$. Also

$$\sigma_P = \frac{0.01}{0.08}(1 - e^{-4 \times 0.08})\sqrt{\frac{1 - e^{-2 \times 0.08 \times 1}}{2 \times 0.08}} = 0.0329$$

and $h = -0.4192$ so that the call price is

$$100 \times 0.6065N(h) - 68 \times 0.9048N(h - \sigma_P) = 0.439$$

21.12. The relevant parameters for the Hull–White model are $a = 0.05$ and $\sigma = 0.015$. Setting $\Delta t = 0.4$

$$\hat{B}(2.1, 3) = \frac{B(2.1, 3)}{B(2.1, 2.5)} \times 0.4 = 0.88888$$

Also from equation (21.23), $\hat{A}(2.1, 3) = 0.99925$ The first stage is to calculate the value of R at time 2.1 years which is such that the value of the bond at that time is 99. Denoting this value of R by R^*, we must solve

$$2.5e^{-R^* \times 0.4} + 102.5\hat{A}(2.1, 3)e^{-\hat{B}(2.1, 3)R^*} = 99$$

The solution to this for R^* turns out to be 6.626%. The option on the coupon bond is decomposed into an option with a strike price of 96.565 on a zero-coupon bond with a principal of 102.5 and an option with a strike price of 2.435 on a zero-coupon bond with a principal of 2.5. The first option is worth 0.0105 and the second option is worth 0.9341. The total value of the option is therefore 0.9446.

21.13. From Section 21.16 the instantaneous futures rate for the Ho–Lee model is

$$G(0,t) = F(0,t) + \frac{\sigma^2 t^2}{2}$$

so that

$$G_t(0,t) = F_t(0,t) + \sigma^2 t$$

This is the expression for $\theta(t)$ in equation (21.13) showing that $G_t(0,t)$ is indeed the drift of the short rate.

21.14. From Section 21.16 the instantaneous futures rate for the Hull-White model is

$$G(0,t) = F(0,t) + \frac{\sigma^2}{2a^2}(1 - e^{-at})^2$$

so that

$$G_t(0,t) = F_t(0,t) + \frac{\sigma^2}{a}(1 - e^{-at})e^{-at}$$

$$G_t(0,t) + a[G(0,t) - r] = F_t(0,t) + aF(0,t) - ar + \frac{\sigma^2}{a}(1 - e^{-at})e^{-at} + \frac{\sigma^2}{2a}(1 - e^{-at})^2$$

$$= F_t(0,t) + aF(0,t) - ar + \frac{\sigma^2}{2a}(1 - e^{-2at})$$

From equation (21.18) this is the same as the drift of r, $\theta(t) - ar$.

21.15. The time step, Δt, is 1 so that $\Delta r = 0.015\sqrt{3} = 0.02598$. Also $j_{\max} = 4$ showing that the branching method should change four steps from the center of the tree. With only three steps we never reach the point where the branching changes. The tree is shown in Figure 21.1.

21.16. A two-year zero-coupon bond pays off \$100 at the ends of the final branches. At node B it is worth $100e^{-0.12 \times 1} = 88.69$. At node C it is worth $100e^{-0.10 \times 1} = 90.48$. At node D it is worth $100e^{-0.08 \times 1} = 92.31$. It follows that at node A the bond is worth

$$(88.69 \times 0.25 + 90.48 \times 0.5 + 92.31 \times 0.25)e^{-0.1 \times 1} = 81.88$$

or \$81.88

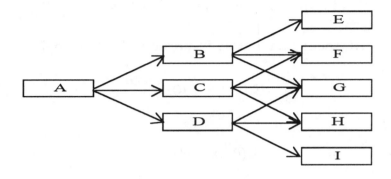

Node	A	B	C	D	E	F	G	H	I
r	10.00%	12.61%	10.01%	7.41%	15.24%	12.64%	10.04%	7.44%	4.84%
p_u	0.1667	0.1429	0.1667	0.1929	0.1217	0.1429	0.1667	0.1929	0.2217
p_m	0.6666	0.6642	0.6666	0.6642	0.6567	0.6642	0.6666	0.6642	0.6567
p_d	0.1667	0.1929	0.1667	0.1429	0.2217	0.1929	0.1667	0.1429	0.1217

Figure 21.1   Tree for Problem 21.15.

21.17. A two-year zero-coupon bond pays off \$100 at time two years. At node B it is worth $100e^{-0.0693 \times 1} = 93.30$. At node C it is worth $100e^{-0.0520 \times 1} = 94.93$. At node D it is worth $100e^{-0.0347 \times 1} = 96.59$. It follows that at node A the bond is worth

$$(93.30 \times 0.167 + 94.93 \times 0.666 + 96.59 \times 0.167)e^{-0.0382 \times 1} = 91.37$$

or \$91.37. The initial two-year rate is $0.08 - 0.05e^{-0.18 \times 2} = 0.0451$ which gives the price of a two-year bond as 91.37. Since $91.37 = e^{-0.04512 \times 2}$, the price of the two-year bond agrees with the initial term structure.

21.18. An 18-month zero-coupon bond pays off \$100 at the final nodes of the tree. At node E it is worth $100e^{-0.088 \times 0.5} = 95.70$. At node F it is worth $100e^{-0.0648 \times 0.5} = 96.81$. At node G it is worth $100e^{-0.0477 \times 0.5} = 97.64$. At node H it is worth $100e^{-0.0351 \times 0.5} = 98.26$. At node I it is worth $100e^{0.0259 \times 0.5} = 98.71$. At node B it is worth

$$(0.118 \times 95.70 + 0.654 \times 96.81 + 0.228 \times 97.64)e^{-0.0564 \times 0.5} = 94.17$$

Similarly at nodes C and D it is worth 95.60 and 96.68. The value at node A is therefore

$$(0.167 \times 94.17 + 0.666 \times 95.60 + 0.167 \times 96.68)e^{-0.0343 \times 0.5} = 93.92$$

The 18-month zero rate is $0.08 - 0.05e^{-0.18 \times 1.5} = 0.0418$. This gives the price of the 18-month zero-coupon bond as $100e^{-0.0418 \times 1.5} = 93.92$ showing that the tree agrees with the initial term structure.

21.19. With 100 time steps the lognormal model gives prices of 5.569, 2.433, and 0.699 for strike prices of 95, 100, and 105. With 100 time steps the normal model gives prices of 5.493, 2.511, and 0.890 for the three strike prices respectively. The normal model gives a fatter left tail and thinner right tail than the lognormal model for interest rates . This translates into a thinner left tail and fatter right tail for bond prices. The arguments in chapter 17 show that we expect the normal model to give higher option prices for high strike prices and lower option prices for low strike. This is indeed what we find.

21.20. The option prices are 0.1302, 0.0814, 0.0580, and 0.0274. The implied Black volatilities are 14.28%, 13.64%, 13.24%, and 12.81%

21.21. When t_2 approaches t_1, $B(t_1, t_2)$ approaches zero and $B(t_1, t_2)/(t_2 - t_1)$ approaches 1.0. The convexity adjustment in equation (21.32) becomes

$$\frac{\sigma^2 B(0, t)^2}{2}$$

where t is the common value of t_1 and t_2. The instantaneous futures rate is therefore

$$F(0, t) + \frac{\sigma^2}{2a^2}(1 - e^{-at})^2$$

From equation (21.27) this is the same as $\alpha(t)$. This is what we would expect since $\alpha(t)$ is the expected short term interest rate in the traditional risk-neutral world and the futures price of a variable equals its expected future spot price in this world.

CHAPTER 22
Interest Rate Derivatives: More Advanced Models

22.1. (a) The expected growth rate of $P(t,T)$ in a risk-neutral world is r. Using Ito's lemma to determine the volatility components we get

$$dP(t,T) = rP(t,T)\,dt + \frac{\partial P(t,T)}{\partial r}\sigma_1\,dz_1 + \frac{\partial P(t,T)}{\partial u}\sigma_2\,dz_2$$

From equation (22.2) this becomes

$$dP(t,T) = rP(t,T)\,dt - B(t,T)P(t,T)\sigma_1\,dz_1 - C(t,T)P(t,T)\sigma_2\,dz_2$$

(b) Define $R(t,T)$ as the bond yield. Since

$$R(t,T) = -\frac{1}{T-t}\ln[P(t,T)]$$

we can use Ito's lemma (or Taylor Series expansion) to obtain

$$dR(t,T) = -\frac{1}{T-t}\left[r - B(t,T)^2\sigma_1^2/2 - C(t,T)^2\sigma_2^2/2 - \rho B(t,T)C(t,T)\sigma_1\sigma_2\right]\,dt$$

$$+\frac{1}{T-t}B(t,T)\sigma_1\,dz_1 + \frac{1}{T-t}C(t,T)\sigma_2\,dz_2$$

(c) Define $B(t,t+T_1)$ as B_1, $B(t,t+T_2)$ as B_2, $C(t,t+T_1)$ as C_1, and $C(t,t+T_2)$ as C_2. The correlation between the T_2 and T_1 rates are

$$\frac{B_1 B_2 \sigma_1^2 + C_1 C_2 \sigma_2^2 + \rho B_1 C_2 \sigma_1\sigma_2 + \rho B_2 C_1 \sigma_1\sigma_2}{\sqrt{(B_1^2\sigma_1^2 + C_1^2\sigma_2^2 + 2\rho B_1 C_1 \sigma_1\sigma_2)(B_2^2\sigma_2^2 + C_2^2\sigma_2^2 + 2\rho B_2 C_2 \sigma_1\sigma_2)}}$$

For the data in Figure 22.1

$$B(t,t+0.25) = 1 - e^{-0.25} = 0.2212$$

$$B(t,t+10) = 1 - e^{-10} = 0.99955$$

$$C(t,t+0.25) = \frac{1}{0.9}e^{-0.25} - \frac{1}{0.1\times 0.9}e^{-0.1\times 0.25} + 10 = 0.02856$$

$$C(t,t+10) = \frac{1}{0.9}e^{-10} - \frac{1}{0.1\times 0.9}e^{-0.1\times 10} + 10 = 5.9125$$

The correlation between the three-month rate and the ten-year rate can be calculated from the above formula as 0.765.

22.2. In a Markov model the expected change and volatility of the short rate at time t depend only on the value of the short rate at time t. In a non-Markov model they depend on the history of the short rate prior to time t.

22.3. Using the notation in section 22.2, when s is constant, $v_T(t, T) = s$, $v_{TT}(t, T) = 0$. Integrating $v_T(t, T)$

$$v(t, T) = sT + \alpha(t)$$

for some function α. Using the fact that $v(T, T) = 0$, we must have

$$v(t, T) = s(T - t)$$

Substituting into equation (22.9) we get

$$dr = F_t(0, t)\, dt + \left[\int_0^t s^2 d\tau \right] dt + s\, dz(t)$$

or

$$dr = [F_t(0, t) + s^2 t]\, dt + s\, dz$$

This is the Ho-Lee model as given by equations (21.12) and (21.13).

22.4. Using the notation in section 22.2, when $v_T(t, T) = s(t, T) = \sigma e^{-a(T-t)}$ so that $v_{TT}(t, T) = -a\sigma e^{-a(T-t)}$. Integrating $v_T(t, T)$

$$v(t, T) = -\frac{1}{a}\sigma e^{-a(T-t)} + \alpha(t)$$

for some function α. Using the fact that $v(T, T) = 0$, we must have

$$v(t, T) = \frac{\sigma}{a}[1 - e^{-a(T-t)}] = \sigma B(t, T)$$

In this case

$$v_{tt}(\tau, t) = -a v_t(\tau, t)$$

so that combining equation (22.9) with equation (22.8), we get

$$dr = F_t(0, t)\, dt + \left\{ \int_0^t [v(\tau, t)v_{tt}(\tau, t) + v_t(\tau, t)^2] d\tau \right\} dt + a[F(0, t) - r(t)]\, dt$$

$$+ a\left[\int_0^t v(\tau, t)v_t(\tau, t) d\tau \right] dt + \sigma\, dz(t)$$

155

Substituting for $v(t, T)$, this reduces to

$$dr = F_t(0, t)\, dt + a[F(0, t) - r(t)]\, dt + \left[\int_0^t e^{-2a(t-\tau)}\, d\tau\right] dt + \sigma\, dz(t)$$

so that

$$dr = F_t(0, t)\, dt + a[F(0, t) - r(t)]\, dt + \frac{1}{2a}[1 - e^{-2at}]\, dt + \sigma\, dz(t)$$

This is the result in equations (21.17) and (21.18).

22.5. When $v(t, T) = x(t)[y(T) - y(t)]$, the component of the drift in the second term in equation (22.9) is a function only of t. Also

$$v_{tt}(\tau, t) = x(\tau)y_t t(t)$$

and

$$v_t(\tau, t) = x(\tau)y_t(t)$$

so that, using equation (22.8), the third term becomes

$$\frac{y_{tt}(t)}{y_t(t)}\left[r(t) - F(0, t) - \int_0^t v(\tau, t)v_t(\tau, t)\, d\tau\right] dt$$

This is a function only of r and t. The coefficient of $dz(t)$ is a function only of t. It follows that the process for r is Markov.

22.6. A ratchet cap tends to provide relatively low payoffs if a high (low) interest rate at one reset date is followed by a high (low) interest rate at the next reset date. High payoffs occur when a low interest rate is followed by a high interest rate. As the number of factors increase, the correlation between successive forward rates declines and there is a greater chance that a low interest rate will be followed by a high interest rate.

22.7. Equation (22.18) can be written

$$dF_k(t) = \zeta_k(t)F_k(t)\sum_{i=m(t)}^k \frac{\delta_i F_i(t)\zeta_i(t)}{1 + \delta_i F_i(t)} + \zeta_k(t)F_k(t)\, dz$$

As δ_i tends to zero, $\zeta_i(t)F_i(t)$ becomes the standard deviation of the instantaneous t_i-maturity forward rate at time t. Using the notation of equation (22.7) this is $s(t, t_i)$. As δ_i tends to zero

$$\sum_{i=m(t)}^k \frac{\delta_i F_i(t)\zeta_i(t)}{1 + \delta_i F_i(t)}$$

156

tends to

$$\int_{\tau=t}^{t_k} s(t, \tau) \, d\tau$$

Equation (22.18) therefore becomes

$$dF_k(t) = s(t, t_k) \int_{\tau=t}^{t_k} s(t, \tau) \, d\tau + s(t, t_k) \, dz$$

This is the HJM result in equation (22.7)

22.8. In a ratchet cap, the cap rate equals the previous reset rate, R, plus a spread. [In the notation of the text it is $R_k + s$.] In a sticky cap the cap rate equal the previous capped rate plus a spread. (In the notation of the text it is $\min(R_k, X_k) + s$.) The strike price in a ratchet cap is always at least a great as that in a sticky cap. Since the value of a cap is a decreasing function of the cap rate, it follows that a sticky cap is more expensive.

22.9. When prepayments increase, the principal is received sooner. This increases the value of a PO. When prepayments increase, less interest is received. This decreases the value of an IO.

22.10. A bond yield is the discount rate that causes the bond's price to equal the market price. The same discount rate is used for all maturities. An OAS is the parallel shift to the Treasury zero curve that causes the price of an instrument such as a mortgage-backed security to equal its market price.

CHAPTER 23
Credit Risk

23.1. The proportional of the no-default value lost between years three and six is $e^{-0.005 \times 3} - e^{-0.008 \times 6} = 0.0320$ or 3.2%.

23.2. When default risk is taken into account, the correct price is $e^{-0.01 \times 3} = 0.9704$ times the Black–Scholes price. The Black–Scholes model therefore overstates the value of the option by $0.0296/0.9704$ or 3.05%.

23.3. Assume that defaults happen only at the end of the life of the forward contract. In a default-free world the forward contract is the combination of a long European call and a short European put where the strike price of the options equals the delivery price and the maturity of the options equals the maturity of the forward contract. If the no-default value of the contract is positive at maturity, the call has a positive value and the put is worth zero. The impact of defaults on the forward contract is the same as that on the call. If the no-default value of the contract is negative at maturity, the call has a zero value and the put has a positive value. In this case defaults have no effect. Again the impact of defaults on the forward contract is the same as that on the call. It follows that the contract has a value equal to a long position in a call that is subject to default risk and short position in a default-free put.

23.4. Suppose that the forward contract provides a payoff at time T. With our usual notation, the value of a long forward contract is $S_T - Ke^{-rT}$. The credit exposure on a long forward contract is therefore $\max(S_T - Ke^{-rT}, 0)$; that is, it is a call on the asset price with strike price Ke^{-rT}. Similarly the credit exposure on a short forward contract is $\max(Ke^{-rT} - S_T, 0)$; that is, it is a put on the asset price with strike price Ke^{-rT}. The total credit exposure is, therefore, a straddle with strike price Ke^{-rT}.

23.5. The credit risk on a matched pair of interest rate swaps is $|B_{\text{fixed}} - B_{\text{floating}}|$. As maturity is approached all bond prices tend to par and this tends to zero. The credit risk on a matched pair of currency swaps is $|SB_{\text{foreign}} - B_{\text{fixed}}|$ where S is the exchange rate. The expected value of this tends to increase as the swap maturity is approached because of the uncertainty in S.

23.6. As time passes there is a tendency for the currency which has the lower interest rate to strengthen. This means that a swap where we are receiving this currency will tend to move in the money (i.e., have a positive value). Similarly a swap where we are paying the currency will tend to move out of the money (i.e., have a negative value). From this it follows that our expected exposure on the swap where we are receiving the low-interest currency is much greater than our expected exposure on the swap where we are receiving the high-interest currency. We should therefore look for counterparties with a low credit risk on the side of the swap where we are receiving the low-interest currency. On the other side of the swap we are far less concerned about the creditworthiness of the counterparty.

23.7. No, put–call parity does not hold when there is default risk. Suppose c^* and p^* are the no-default prices of a European call and put with strike price X and maturity T on a non-dividend-paying stock whose price is S, and that c and p are the corresponding values when there is default risk. The text shows that when we make the independence assumption, $c = c^* e^{-[y(T)-y^*(T)]T}$ and $p = p^* e^{-[y(T)-y^*(T)]T}$. The relationship

$$c^* + Xe^{-y^*(T)T} = p^* + S$$

which holds in a no-default world therefore becomes

$$c + Xe^{-y(T)T} = p + Se^{-[y(T)-y^*(T)]T}$$

when there is default risk. This is not the same a regular put–call parity. What is more, the relationship depends on the independence assumption and cannot be deduced from the same sort of simple no-arbitrage arguments that we used in Chapter 7 for the put–call parity relationship in a no-default world.

23.8. Total return swaps can be used to get rid of a credit risk or to achieve credit risk diversification. If a company agrees to pay the return on assets that it owns and to receive either a fixed or floating rate of interest, it passes the credit risk asociated with the assets to the counterparty. If it agrees to pay the return on the assets it owns and receive the return on other assets subject to credit risk, it is exchanging one credit risk for another. This might be part of a credit risk diversification strategy.

23.9. A credit default swap could be structured so that 120 basis points is paid to a counterparty each year in return for the right to sell the reference bond to the counterparty for its face value. This ignores the possibility of the counterparty defaulting. It also ignores the possibility that, in the event of a default, the price of the reference bond may be artifically high because all companies with credit default swaps on the bond will try to buy it. Finally, the analysis assumes that the no-default value of the bond is par at the time of default. It is likely that the no-default value of the bond is greater than par because it has a relatively high coupon. All of these points suggest that the actual annual payment should be less than 120 basis points.

23.10. The statements in (a) and (b) are true. The statement in (c) is not. Suppose that v_X and v_Y are the exposures to X and Y. The expected value of $v_X + v_Y$ is the expected value of v_X plus the expected value of v_Y. The same is not true of 95% confidence limits.

23.11. It is possible that a new transaction tends to offset existing transactions with the counterparty. Its incremental effect is then likely to be that of reducing credit risk when netting is allowed.

23.12. The gradients indicate that on average we expect the creditworthiness of a BBB to decline faster than that of a AAA. When a company borrows a floating rate of interest and swaps it to fixed rate of interest, it is, as explained in chapter 5, subject to rollover risk. The rollover risk is much higher for the BBB than for the AAA. This explains why a BBB often appears to have a comparative advantage (relative to a AAA) in floating-rate markets.

23.13. The cost of defaults is uv where u is the probability of a default during the life of the contract and v is the value of an option that pays off $\max(150S_T - 100, 0)$ in one year and S_T is the value in dollars of one AUD. The value of u is

$$u = 1 - e^{-(0.06-0.05)\times 1} = 0.009950$$

The variable v is 150 times a call option to buy one AUD for 0.6667. The formula for the call option in terms of forward prices is

$$[FN(d_1) - XN(d_2)]e^{-rT}$$

where

$$d_1 = \frac{\log(F/X) + \sigma^2 T/2}{\sigma\sqrt{T}}$$

$$d_2 = d_1 - \sigma\sqrt{T}$$

In this case $F = 0.6667$, $X = 0.6667$, $\sigma = 0.12$, $T = 1$, and $r = 0.05$ so that $d_1 = 0.06, d_2 = -0.06$ and the value of the call option is 0.0303. It follows that $v = 150 \times 0.0303 = 4.545$ so that the cost of defaults is

$$4.545 \times 0.009950 = 0.04522$$

23.14. In this case the costs of defaults is $u_1 v_1 + u_2 v_2$ where

$$u_1 = 1 - e^{-(0.055-0.05)\times 0.5} = 0.002497$$

$$u_2 = e^{-(0.055-0.05)\times 0.5} - e^{-(0.06-0.05)\times 1} = 0.007453$$

v_1 is the value of an option that pays off $\max(150S_T - 100, 0)$ in six months and v_2 is the value of a option that pays off $\max(150S_T - 100, 0)$ in one year. The calculations in Problem 23.13 show that v_2 is 4.545. Similarly $v_1 = 3.300$ so that the cost of defaults is

$$0.002497 \times 3.300 + 0.007453 \times 4.545 = 0.04211$$

23.15. In this case $\sigma = 0.25$, $\Delta t = 0.5$, $r = 0.06$ and the tree parameters are $u = 1.1934$, $d = 0.8380$, $a = 1.0305$, $p = 0.5416$, and $1 - p = 0.4584$. The tree is shown in Figure 23.1. The top number at each node is the stock price; the second number is the value of the equity component of the convertible; the third number is the value of the debt component; the fourth number is the total value of the convertible. At node G and H the bond should be converted and is worth five times the stock price. At nodes I and J it should not be converted and is worth \$100. At node D the equity component is 142.41 and the debt component zero. (Neither calling nor converting change the value at this node.) At node E the value of the equity component is

$$0.5416 \times 119.34 \times e^{-0.06 \times 0.5} = 62.72$$

and the value of the debt component is

$$0.4584 \times 100 \times e^{-0.1 \times 0.5} = 43.60$$

The total value of the convertible is 106.32. The bond should be neither converted nor called at this node. At node F the convertible is worth $100e^{-0.1 \times 0.5} = 95.12$. Again it should be neither called nor converted. At node B, the value of the equity component is

$$(0.5416 \times 142.41 + 0.4584 \times 62.72)e^{-0.06 \times 0.5} = 105.88$$

The value of the debt component is

$$0.4584 \times 43.60 \times e^{-0.1 \times 0.5} = 19.01$$

The total value of the convertible is therefore 124.89. In this case the bond should be called. The holder can either take the 110 call price or convert into $5 \times 23.87 = 119.34$ of equity. The latter is the better alternative. The result of these calculations is therefore that the bond is worth 119.34, all of it equity, at node B. At node C the equity component is

$$0.5416 \times 62.72 \times e^{-0.06 \times 0.5} = 32.97$$

The debt component is

$$(0.5416 \times 43.60 + 0.4584 \times 95.12)e^{-0.1 \times 0.5} = 63.94$$

The total value at this node is 96.91 and the bond should be neither converted nor called. The value of the equity component at the initial node, A, is

$$(0.5416 \times 119.34 + 0.4584 \times 32.97)e^{-0.06 \times 0.5} = 77.39$$

The value of the debt component is

$$0.4584 \times 63.94 \times e^{-0.1 \times 0.5} = 27.88$$

The initial value of the convertible is therefore 105.27. The value of the bond without the conversion option is $100e^{-0.1 \times 1.5} = 86.07$. The value of the conversion option (net of the issuer's call option) is therefore $105.27 - 86.07 = 19.20$.

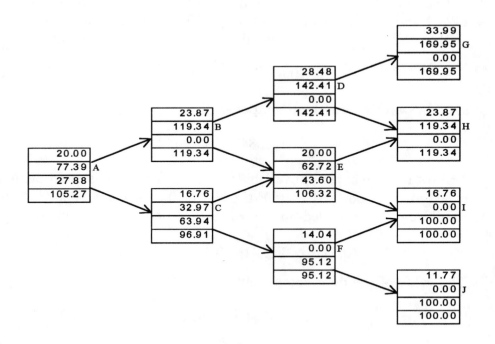

Figure 23.1   Tree for Problem 23.15.